CA Proficiency 1

FINANCIAL ACCOUNTING TOOLKIT

Published in 2013 by
Chartered Accountants Ireland
Chartered Accountants House
47-47 Pearse Street
Dublin 2
www.charteredaccountants.ie

© The Institute of Chartered Accountants in Ireland 2013

First published 2007
Updated 2009, 2011 and 2013

Copyright in this publication is owned by The Institute of Chartered Accountants in Ireland. All rights reserved. No part of this text may be reproduced or transmitted or communicated to the public in any form or by any means, including photocopying, Internet or e-mail dissemination, without the written permission of The Institute of Chartered Accountants in Ireland. Such written permission must also be obtained before any part of this document is stored in a retrieval system of any nature.

This publication is designed to provide accurate and authoritative information in regard to the subject matter covered. It is provided on the understanding that The Institute of Chartered Accountants in Ireland is not engaged in rendering professional services. The Institute of Chartered Accountants in Ireland disclaims all liability for any reliance placed on the information contained within this publication and recommends that, if professional advice or other expert assistance is required, the services of a competent professional should be sought.

ISBN: 978-1-908199-69-0

Typeset by Deanta Global Publishing Services
Printed by CPI Group Ltd

CONTENTS

		Page
	Introduction	v
Section One:	**Sole Trader: Jane Dough – The Dough House**	1
Section Two:	**Partnership: The Poulenc Partnership**	11
Section Three:	**Limited Company: My Company Limited (MCL)**	19
Section Four:	**Group: The Pot Limited Group (Pot Ltd)**	47
	Suggested Solutions	61

INTRODUCTION

Please read the CAP 1 Competency Statement carefully, in particular those aspects relating to Paper 3 Financial Accounting. The purpose of this Toolkit is to equip students with an understanding of the context of financial accounting in the business environment, and to provide fundamental accounting capabilities. The broad structure of the Toolkit is as follows:

- Section One – Jane Dough: The Dough House – addresses the fundamental principles that underlie financial accounting and the preparation of sole trader accounts.
- Section Two – Poulenc Partnership – focuses on the basic principles that underlie partnership accounting and the preparation of partnership accounts, including partnership changes and the conversion of a partnership to a limited company.
- Section Three – My Company Limited (MCL) – concentrates on preparation and presentation of financial statements of companies.
- Section Four – Pot Limited Group (Pot Ltd) – focuses on the preparation and presentation of consolidated financial statements.

This edition of the Toolkit has been fully revised and incorporates, for example, the revisions to IAS 1 *Presentation of Financial Statements* which, among other things, include the adoption of the title 'Statement of Profit or Loss and Other Comprehensive Income' (SPLOCI) in preference to Statement of Comprehensive Income (SoCI). This is explained more fully in Section Three. While IAS 1 still permits the use of other titles (for example, SoCI), this Toolkit applies the designation SPLOCI in Section Three and Section Four, which deal with the preparation of company and consolidated financial statements respectively. Given the nature of sole trader (Section One) and partnership (Section Two) financial statements, it is considered appropriate to continue to use terms such as 'income statement' and 'cash flow statement' in these sections.

USING THE TOOLKIT

As part of the CA Proficiency 1 course, you are invited here to take on the role of 'Chris', a fictitious trainee Chartered Accountant. Chris's job entails specific responsibilities for three clients, detailed below. As you work through the material in each of the subject-areas, you will be asked to attempt tasks presented to Chris on behalf of each of these clients. These tasks are designed to help you apply the knowledge and skills required for your professional examinations.

You should treat these simulations as though they are real-life tasks. Try and put yourself in Chris's position – considering how you might respond to the client, where you might go to get information and when you might ask for help. While some of the tasks will be completed within the lecture setting, others will be available for you to complete in your own time. Watch out for the signposts on these tasks: often they will refer you to some necessary pre-reading. In addition, the signposts will also note where you can find supplementary questions.

Chris's Background

You are Chris, a trainee accountant with Shield Kenwick, Chartered Accountants & Registered Auditors. Your manager is one of the partners, Mr Ryan. You have just received the following memo from Mr Ryan.

**SHIELD KENWICK
CHARTERED ACCOUNTANTS &
REGISTERED AUDITORS**

INTERNAL MEMO

Date: dd/mm/yy
To: Chris
From: Mr Ryan
Re: Update following six-month review meeting

At your recent review meeting we agreed that you are ready to take on some extra responsibility and that you should have further direct exposure to clients. I have considered how this might be best achieved, and have decided the following:

Jane Dough – The Dough House

Jane Dough is a new client, starting up a new business. As part of your duties, you will be the first point of contact and reference for any queries from Jane. In particular, you will be responsible for the preparation of Jane's books and records, income tax, PAYE and VAT returns. I will sign these off in the usual way. I have included background notes on Jane in **Appendix 1**. Jane also mentioned that she is interested in the activities of a local producers group, called Poulenc Partnership. I have included their details in **Appendix 2**, in case you require them at a later point.

> **My Company Limited**
>
> As part of your duties, you will be seconded one day per week as assistant management accountant to a busy manufacturing company that is a client of the firm. Shield Kenwick provides general support and advice, along with accounting and taxation services, to this client. We do not carry out the statutory audit. The company, My Company Limited (MCL), is family owned and you will report directly to the Finance Director, Mike Smithers, while at the office. Additionally, I would hope that you will come directly to me with specific queries which you might like to discuss. I have included some basic background information on MCL in **Appendix 3**.
>
> I anticipate that these responsibilities should help to address some of the areas of concern we had in relation to the competencies identified in the Online CA Diary. I suggest we keep the process under review over the next six to 12 months.
>
> **The Pot Limited Group**
>
> In working with Jane Dough and the Poulenc Partnership, you will have gained valuable experience in the preparation and presentation of financial statements for a sole trader and a partnership, both of which are not subject to company law and international accounting standards.
>
> Having dealt with Jane Dough, the Poulenc Partnership and MCL, and therefore with:
>
> - the prime books of original entry;
> - the preparation and presentation of financial statements for a sole trader and a partnership; and
> - the preparation and presentation of financial statements for a limited company,
>
> I feel that you will now be in a position to advance your training by joining my audit team which has a portfolio of groups of companies. Your initial focus will be on the preparation of a consolidated statement of financial position for the Pot Limited Group, details of which you will find in **Appendix 4**. You will need to become familiar with the terminology pertaining to groups as well as the fundamental principles and practices relating to the preparation of consolidated accounts.

Having agreed to Mr Ryan's suggestions, you return to your desk and continue your work.

> **Appendix 1: Jane Dough – The Dough House**
>
> On 1 January 2012, Jane Dough established a new business, a coffee and pastry shop, known as 'The Dough House'. In the future, Jane hopes to also sell local pottery and produce on a small scale. Jane had identified suitable premises in a busy part of town that did not appear to be particularly well serviced by coffee and pastry shops. While Jane has extensive experience working in a coffee shop environment,

having been assistant manager in a similar shop for several years, she has never owned or run her own business before.

On 1 January 2012, Jane withdrew €/£5,000 from her own savings and John's great-aunt gave her €/£10,000 as a gift to put towards opening The Dough House. Jane opened a separate bank account for The Dough House, lodging €/£14,500 to the account and retaining €/£500 as petty cash. Jane then signed the deeds on The Dough House's new premises, which were for sale at €/£50,000, drew down a mortgage with a local Building Society for €/£45,000 and paid the balance due for the premises from the business's new bank account. The mortgage is repayable over 20 years and the repayments, which are due at the end of each month, are fixed at €/£250 per month.

While Jane had taken redundancy from her previous employer, the redundancy payment is not expected for some months due to circumstances outside her control.

Jane will need help at lunchtime and weekends in The Dough House, and her nephew and niece have agreed to help, so long as they are paid in cash. They are 14 and 17 respectively. Additionally, Jane's husband John has agreed to help whenever possible. Jane is uncertain whether she needs to register as an employer.

Jane and John have two young children, and her husband's incapacitated great-aunt lives with them. John is not employed as he cares for their two children on a full-time basis at home. However, he does have an interest in some rental properties and a small share portfolio. Jane and John have always tried to save a percentage of their income and these savings are kept in a variety of accounts: Credit Union Account, Deposit Account and SSIA. In addition, Jane and John each have a personal pension, life assurance (with critical illness) and are members of Vhi.

Appendix 2: The Poulenc Partnership

The Poulenc Partnership is a group of artisans who make and sell local produce and crafts through farmers' markets, seasonal fairs and independent coffee shops. The partnership has been in existence for approximately eight years and there are currently five partners. The partners share all income and costs, with individual products being sold into the partnership at an agreed price and then sold on to third parties. The current partnership structure is as follows:

- Maire Louise Phillips (25%) – potter and clay-worker;
- Joseph Phillips (father of Maire Louise) (15%) – basket weaver;
- Christopher Pringle (20%) – food producer (preserves, cakes, biscuits, etc.) using local ingredients;
- Caiti Pollen (25%) – craft worker (jewellery from local materials and wrought iron items (candlesticks, tables, fire irons, etc.); and
- Ellen Peterson (15%) – public relations and marketing professional, and the only partner who draws a salary.

While Joseph Phillips hopes to retire during 2013, he may continue to sell some of his baskets to the partnership.

Jane has been invited to join The Poulenc Partnership, with effect from 1 July 2013, purchasing Joseph Phillips's 15% interest in return for an investment of €/£50,000.

As The Poulenc Partnership is now a client of the firm, Jane has deferred making a decision about joining the partnership until its accounts for the year ended 31 December 2012 have been finalised.

The existing partners have indicated that there are plans to review the partnership structure at the end of 2013.

Appendix 3: My Company Limited

My Company Limited (MCL) is a large, privately-owned company. It was founded in the 1970s by Matthew Smithers and is still owned by the Smithers family. There has been no change in the ordinary share capital of the company for a number of years and the shareholdings are as follows:

Member	Role	Current Shareholding
Matthew and Maureen Smithers	Founders	8%
Matthew Jnr	CEO	22%
Michael	Finance Director	22%
Martina	Production Director	22%
Millie	Sales and Marketing Director	22%
Mervin (based in New York)	Not involved in the company	4%

All of the above members are also directors.

Matthew Jnr, Michael, Martina and Millie are the only children of Matthew and Maureen. There are no other directors.

MCL is a textiles company that is involved in producing standard fabric dyes and weaving natural fibre fabrics for use in a variety of home furnishings. The dyes produced are used to dye yarns in-house (but could also be sold directly to third parties). The majority of the woven fabrics are exported to the UK and mainland Europe. However, there is also a core Irish market.

MCL has a large work force that includes: general operatives; weavers (general and skilled); stores team; administration team; and sales and distribution team. Although the company has performed well in the past, it has come under increasing pressure in the last two years.

> **Appendix 4: The Pot Limited Group**
>
> Pot Ltd is a private company which was incorporated in 2000. The company is involved in wholesaling food, kitchen supplies and hardware to the hotel and catering industry. Pot Ltd has traded very successfully since incorporation and has accumulated significant retained earnings. The company has a board of directors of six members, one of which is both chairman and chief executive officer.
>
> In 2011, Pot Ltd acquired a large controlling interest in Stew Ltd, a company which has a chain of fast food outlets throughout Ireland. Stew Ltd has grown significantly, particularly in the immediate years before the acquisition and is now very well placed to expand by entering the UK market. Each company has its own financial controller and accounts department and both are well equipped as regards management information systems and state-of-the-art computing facilities.

COMMON ABBREVIATIONS

IAS	International Accounting Standard
IASB	International Accounting Standards Board
IFRS	International Financial Reporting Standard
JNL	Journal
NA	Net Assets
PAT	Profit After Tax
PBT	Profit Before Tax
PDB	Purchase Day Book
RE	Retained Earnings
SDB	Sales Day Book
SoCE	Statement of Changes in Equity
SoCI	Statement of Comprehensive Income
SoFP	Statement of Financial Position
SPLOCI	Statement of Profit or Loss and Other Comprehensive Income
TB	Trial Balance

Section One

SOLE TRADER:
JANE DOUGH – THE DOUGH HOUSE

INTRODUCTION

By the end of Section One, with respect to the financial accounting aspects of the CA Proficiency 1 course, you should:

- be familiar with the fundamental principles which underlie financial accounting;
- be able to explain the types of information which must be recorded to obtain a set of sole trader accounts;
- be able to record transactions in books of prime entry and extract to trial balance using double entry book-keeping; and
- have the ability to prepare and present interim and/or end-of-year sole trader accounts.

[It is important to remember that the format and presentation of the accounts dealt with in Section One (income statement and statement of financial position) do not adhere strictly to those outlined in Section Three and Section Four which address limited company and consolidated financial statements respectively.]

Meeting 1 – 1 January 2012

Task 1

Jane asked you to explain the fundamental principles which underlie accounting and prepare a statement showing the opening financial position of The Dough House (using the information provided by Mr Ryan).

*[Before responding to Jane's request you should read the section on the Conceptual Framework for Financial Reporting in Chapter 1: Framework for Financial Reporting of your core textbook (*International Financial Accounting and Reporting (4th Edition) *by Ciaran Connolly* **(Connolly)**, *together with Part 1, Section One of the* Double Entry Book-keeping Toolkit.*]*

Meeting 2 – End of Week 1, 2012

During the first week of trading, Jane purchased goods on credit for sale in the business at a cost of €/£1,000. She also purchased fixtures and fittings amounting to €/£2,500, paying for them by cheque. At the end of the first week, till receipts amounted to €/£1,350 and goods that had originally cost €/£100 remained unsold. All receipts were lodged to the bank at the end of each day's business, with the exception of €/£200 that Jane kept so that her family could go out and celebrate a successful first week. While Jane had been able to cope during the first week without any additional help, she realised that this could not continue.

Task 2

Jane has asked you to prepare a statement showing the financial position of The Dough House at the end of the first week of trading.

[Before responding to Jane's request you should read Part 1, Section One of the Double Entry Book-keeping Toolkit *and attempt the Self-test Questions.]*

Meeting 3 – End of Week 3, 2012

Jane believes that The Dough House has performed well in the two weeks since your last meeting. However, she has been very busy with other aspects of the business and has had to rely upon hired staff more than she expected. Based upon your advice and guidance, she has kept the business's records up-to-date and has provided you with the following information as at the end of week 3:

- there were no additions to the premises or fixtures and fittings;
- the cost of inventory held is €/£80, after deducting foodstuffs costing €/£20 which were used at home;
- cash at bank €/£8,000;
- cash-in-hand €/£400;
- amount owing to suppliers for goods purchased for resale €/£850; and
- she had withdrawn €/£250 in both week 2 and week 3 for her own use and had not introduced any of her own money into the business. The first payment on the mortgage was due at the end of week 4.

Task 3

Jane has asked you whether The Dough House made a profit in weeks 2 and 3.

Meeting 4 – End of Month 2, 2012

Jane has informed you that not only does business continue to be strong at The Dough House, but she has been successful in obtaining a number of contracts with local companies to supply tea, coffee, soup and sandwiches for lunchtime meetings and events in their offices. While Jane is confident that the contracts are profitable, she is concerned about maintaining proper records as the contract sales are on credit and the business's credit purchases have increased correspondingly.

Jane has summarised the business's sales and purchases during the first two months as follows:

1. Bought goods from Country Foods Limited, a supplier, for €/£1,000 on credit.
2. Cash sales €/£1,350.
3. Bought goods from Fine Fare Limited, another supplier, for €1,500 on credit.
4. Cash sales €/£2,000.
5. Bought goods from Country Foods Limited and Fine Fare Limited for €/£1,200 and €/£1,400 respectively on credit.
6. Sold goods to Cartwright Limited, a customer, for €/£2,200 on credit.
7. Cash Sales €/£1,400.
8. Paid Country Foods Limited €/£1,000 for goods purchased on credit.
9. Paid Fine Fare Limited €/£1,500 for goods purchased on credit.
10. Received €/£2,200 cash from Cartwright Limited.
11. Bought goods from Country Foods Limited for €/£3,300 on credit.
12. Sold goods to Corpus Limited, a customer, for €/£2,500 on credit.
13. Cash sales €/£2,300.
14. Paid Country Foods Limited and Fine Fare Limited €/£1,200 and €/£1,400 respectively for goods purchased on credit.
15. Bought goods for €/£350 cash.
16. Cash sales €/£600.

Jane has also informed you that the business paid the following expenses during the first two months:

	€/£
Premises (excess over mortgage)	5,000
Fixtures and fittings	2,500
Mortgage repayments	500
Wages	800
Drawings	1,600
	10,400

(Ignore VAT)

Task 4

Jane has asked you to record these transactions in the business's books and records.

[Before responding to Jane's request you should read Part 1, Sections Two and Four of the Double Entry Book-keeping Toolkit, *together with attempting the Self-test Questions.]*

Ethical Dilemma

Mr Ryan calls you to his office and asks you what you would do if two police officers came to the office and asked to see the files of one of your clients who owns a newsagents.

Task 5

What should you do?

Meeting 5 – End of Month 4, 2012

You have been keeping in contact with Jane by telephone and e-mail since your last meeting at the end of February, and all the indications are that the business is developing satisfactorily. However, Jane recently requested your help with some accounting issues she was having difficulty with.

[Before responding to these issues you should read Part 1, Section Four of the Double Entry Book-keeping Toolkit *and attempt the Self-test Questions.]*

Accounting Issue 1

The balance on The Dough House's Sales Ledger Control Account (Receivables Control Account) at the end of April 2012 was €/£9,345. However, when Jane extracted a list of balances from the Sales Ledger (Receivables Ledger), she found that they totalled €/£9,425. On further investigation, she found the errors listed below.

(a) Sales to Corpus Limited of €/£240 have been mistakenly entered on Corpus Limited's individual account in the payables ledger.
(b) An invoice for €/£310 in respect of sales to Cartwright Limited was not recorded in the Sales Day Book.
(c) A contra entry of €/£100 has been made on Mission Limited's individual account in the sales ledger against their account in the payables ledger. This has not been recorded in the control accounts.
(d) A debit balance of €/£400 has been omitted from the list of balances.
(e) An invoice for €/£282 has been correctly entered in the Sales Day Book but posted to the customer's individual account as €/£822.

(f) Cash received from Morricone Limited of €/£500 has not been recorded on his individual ledger account.
(g) The Sales Day Book total was overcast by €/£220.

Task 6

Explain the action required to correct each error; write up an adjusted Sales Ledger Control Account, and reconcile this to the corrected total list of balances.

Accounting Issue 2

The balance on The Dough House's Purchase Ledger Control Account (Payables Control Account) at the end of April 2012 was €/£8,445. However, Jane's extracted list of balances from the Purchase Ledger (Payables Ledger) totalled €/£8,870 and she believes that she may have made some book-keeping errors. The errors identified were:

(a) The Purchases Day Book had been undercast by €/£650.
(b) €/£400 owing to Filler Limited had been settled by a contra entry to their individual receivables ledger account. No entry had been to the control accounts.
(c) An invoice from Country Foods Limited for goods bought from the company had been illegible and could not be entered in the Purchases Day Book. The amount is now known to be €/£850.
(d) Cash paid to Fine Fare Limited of €/£700 had been recorded in the cash book but not in the company's individual ledger account.
(e) A credit balance of €/£450 had been omitted from the list of balances.
(f) Sales to Corpus Limited of €/£240 have been mistakenly entered on Corpus Limited's individual account in the payables ledger.

Task 7

Amend the Purchase Ledger Control Account and list of balances so that they agree.

Accounting Issue 3

The cash book of The Dough House showed a debit balance of €/£8,100 at 30 April 2012. However, the bank statement showed a credit balance of €/£5,650.

After examining the cash book and bank statement for the four-month period since the business started, you have found the following items which need to be adjusted for:

(a) Cheques from customers totalling €/£6,500 were entered in the cash book on 28 April but did not clear the bank until 2 May.
(b) Cheques issued by Jane to pay creditors on 29 April which totalled €/£3,650 did not appear on the bank statement until May.

(c) A direct debit for the Building Society mortgage of €/£250 was paid by the bank on 30 April but no entry had been made for this in the cash book.
(d) A credit transfer for €/£650 had been received by the bank on 30 April from one of The Dough House's customers, but this had not been entered in the cash book.

Task 8

Jane has asked you to prepare a bank reconciliation statement for her.

Ethical Dilemma

Another of your firm's audit clients is a jewellery designer who sells her products from her own store. One day after a meeting you mention that you have to find a special present for your mother's 60th birthday. Your client shows you a pair of diamond earrings set in white gold and says that she can sell them to you for a 'good price'.

Task 9

What should you do?

Meeting 6 – End of Month 6, 2012

At the end of the June 2012, you extracted the following trial balance as at 31 May 2012 from the books and records of The Dough House.

TRIAL BALANCE
as at 31 May 2012

	DR €/£	CR €/£
Premises – at cost	50,000	
Fixtures and fittings – at cost	2,500	
Mortgage (€/£45,000 − (5 × €/£250))		43,750
Drawings	5,100	
Capital		15,000
Bank	8,000	
Cash	500	
Purchases	24,600	
Trade payable – Country Foods Limited		850
Trade payable – Filler Limited		200
Trade payable – Fine Fare Limited		910
Insurance (€/£60 per month)	300	
Sales		34,750
Trade receivable – Cartwright Limited	420	
Trade receivable – Corpus Limited	380	

Trade receivable – Mission Limited	500	
Stationery and advertising	660	
Postage and telephone	150	
Heat and light	250	
Staff wages	2,000	
General expenses	100	
	95,460	95,460

Task 10

Jane has asked you to record the following transactions for the month of June 2012 in the records of The Dough House: balance off the ledger accounts; extract a trial balance as at 30 June 2012; and prepare an income statement for the six-month period ended 30 June 2012 and a balance sheet as at that date.

June 1	Bought goods on credit from: Country Foods Limited €/£400, Filler Limited €/£1,200 and Fine Fare Limited €/£1,350.
June 2	Bought shop fixtures and fittings by cheque €/£500.
June 5	Paid insurance by cheque €/£160.
June 7	Lodged cash sales for week to bank €/£1,580.
June 7	Paid wages by cheque €/£100.
June 7	Sold goods on credit to: Morricone Limited €/£500, Cartwright Limited €/£400 and Corpus Limited €/£300.
June 8	Bought stationery on credit from Ball Limited €/£100.
June 9	Paid postage and telephone by cheque €/£75.
June 10	Paid heat and light by cheque €/£50.
June 11	Returned goods to Filler Limited €/£200.
June 12	Paid Ball Limited by cheque €/£100.
June 13	Sold goods on credit to: Banks Limited €/£220, Cartwright Limited €/£150 and Mission Limited €/£270.
June 14	Lodged cash sales for week to bank €/£1,610.
June 14	Issued credit note for invoicing error to Morricone Limited €/£40.
June 15	Paid wages by cash €/£120.
June 17	Received from Morricone by cheque €/£460.
June 20	Refund for overpaid insurance received by cheque €/£100.
June 21	Paid general expenses by cash €/£50.
June 21	Lodged cash sales for week to bank €/£1,575.
June 21	Paid wages by cheque €/£100.
June 25	Received by cheque from Banks Limited €/£220 and Cartwright Limited €/£100.
June 28	Paid by cheque Filler Limited €/£1,200 and postage and telephone €/£75.
June 28	Lodged cash sales for week to bank €/£1,645.

June 28 Paid wages by cheque €/£100.
June 30 Bought delivery van by cheque €/£6,000.
June 30 Paid mortgage by direct debit €/£250.
June 30 Jane took drawings by cheque €/£1,000.

Jane believes that the cost of goods held for resale at 30 June 2012 was €/£200. (Ignore prepayments, accruals, depreciation and taxation.)

[Before responding to Jane's request, you should read Part 1, Section Four of the Double Entry Book-keeping Toolkit.*]*

Meeting 7 – Early January 2013

In early January 2013, you met with Jane and extracted the following trial balance as at 31 December 2012 from the books and records of The Dough House.

The Dough House
Trial Balance
as at 31 December 2012

	DR €/£	CR €/£
Premises – at cost	50,000	
Delivery van – at cost	6,000	
Fixtures and fittings – at cost	4,000	
Mortgage (€/£45,000 – (12 × €/£250))		42,000
Drawings	16,000	
Capital		15,000
Bank	6,100	
Cash	300	
Purchases	56,400	
Trade payable – Country Foods Limited		1,200
Trade payable – Filler Limited		905
Trade payable – Fine Fare Limited		1,800
Insurance (€/£60 per month)	780	
Sales		89,600
Trade receivable – Cartwright Limited	550	
Trade receivable – Corpus Limited	500	
Trade receivable – Mission Limited	600	
Trade receivable – Other	650	
Stationery and advertising	900	
Postage and telephone	400	
Heat and light	950	
Staff wages	5,775	
General expenses	600	
	150,505	150,505

Jane also provided you with the following information:

1. It is considered appropriate to depreciate the business's non-current assets as follows:

    Premises   – 2% on cost.
    Delivery van   – 25% on cost.
    Fixtures and fittings – 20% on cost.

    Furthermore, it has been agreed that a full year's depreciation should be charged in the year of disposal and none in the year of acquisition.
2. It is expected that approximately 10% of the other trade receivables will not be received.
3. A bill for €/£80 was received in January 2013 in respect of heat and light for December 2012.
4. General expenses include €/£50 relating to items for Jane's own personal use.
5. The cost of goods held for resale at 31 December 2012 was €/£250.

Task 11

Prepare an income statement for the year ended 31 December 2012 and a statement of financial position as at that date. (Ignore taxation.)

[Before responding to Jane's request you should read Part 1, Section Three of the Double Entry Book-keeping Toolkit *and attempt the Self-test Questions.]*

CONCLUSION

Now that you have worked through this Section, you should have formed an understanding of how double entry book-keeping works and be familiar with the main books of account. You should also be able to:

- draw up and balance T accounts;
- extract a trial balance;
- identify income statement balances;
- identify statement of financial position balances;
- draw up an income statement;
- draw up a statement of financial position;
- reconcile control accounts;
- prepare bank reconciliation statements; and
- calculate prepayments and accruals.

This knowledge will form a base from which you can learn how to prepare accounts for partnerships, limited companies and many other types of organisation. You may have found some parts of this Section rather daunting but don't despair, it will become clearer with practice and experience. The main thing to remember is that 'for every debit, there is a corresponding credit'.

[And finally, you should now attempt the Exam Level Questions at the end of Part 1 of the Double Entry Book-keeping Toolkit.]

Section Two

PARTNERSHIP: THE POULENC PARTNERSHIP

INTRODUCTION

By the end of Section Two, with respect to the financial accounting aspects of the CA Proficiency 1 course, you should be able to:

- describe the basic principles which underlie partnership accounting;
- account for partnership changes, including the retirement of existing partners and the admission of new partners;
- prepare partnership accounts, including income statement, statement of financial position and partners' capital accounts; and
- account for the conversion of a partnership to a limited company.

Meeting 1 – 31 January 2013

Following a meeting with Maire Louise Phillips, you have obtained the following information in relation to the Poulenc Partnership for the year ended 31 December 2012:

The Poulenc Partnership
Trial Balance
as at 31 December 2012

	Dr €/£	Cr €/£
Sales		650,000
Inventory at 1 January 2012	78,000	
Purchases	380,000	
Carriage inwards	4,000	
Carriage outwards	5,000	
Trade payables		52,000
Cash at bank	50,000	

Current accounts:		
Maire Louise Phillips		10,000
Joseph Phillips		8,000
Christopher Pringle		7,000
Caiti Pollen		11,000
Ellen Peterson		4,000
Capital accounts:		
Maire Louise Phillips		45,000
Joseph Phillips		40,000
Christopher Pringle		34,000
Caiti Pollen		50,000
Ellen Peterson		26,000
Drawings:		
Maire Louise Phillips	35,000	
Joseph Phillips	25,000	
Christopher Pringle	22,000	
Caiti Pollen	30,000	
Ellen Peterson	18,000	
General expenses	36,000	
Trade receivables	168,000	
Premises – cost as at 1 January 2012	80,000	
Premises – accumulated depreciation as at 1 January 2012		12,000
Fixtures and fittings – cost as at 1 January 2012	24,000	
Fixtures and fittings – accumulated depreciation as at 1 January 2012		6,000
	955,000	955,000

Additional information:

(a) Inventory at 31 December 2012 is valued for accounts purposes at €/£71,000.
(b) Depreciation of €/£2,000 and €/£4,000 is to be provided on the premises and fixtures and fittings respectively.
(c) The profit-sharing arrangements are as follows:
  (i) interest on capital is to be provided at a rate of 10% per annum;
  (ii) Ellen Peterson is to receive a salary of €/£9,500 per annum; and
  (iii) the balance of profit or loss is to be divided between the partners as follows: Maire Louise Phillips (25%); Joseph Phillips (15%); Christopher Pringle (20%); Caiti Pollen (25%); and Ellen Peterson (15%).

Task 12

The partners have requested that you prepare the accounts of The Poulenc Partnership for the year ended 31 December 2012.

[*Before responding to the partners' request, you should read the sections on the Partnership Act 1890 and Basic Principles in* Chapter 36: Accounting for Partnerships of Connolly.]

Ethical Dilemma

Your firm has been approached by a prospective new client, a small subsidiary of an overseas company involved in import/export in a country where your firm has no business contacts.

Task 13

What should your firm do?

Meeting 2 – 28 February 2013

During a meeting with the partners of The Poulenc Partnership to discuss the accounts for the year ended 31 December 2012 and plans for the future of the partnership, Jane Dough was informed that Joseph Phillips had confirmed his desire to retire from the partnership with effect from 1 July 2013. Furthermore, the partners indicated that, while goodwill was not recognised in the partnership accounts, any payment by Jane to join the partnership would include an element in respect of goodwill.

Task 14

Prepare a briefing note for Jane that explains how goodwill is measured and the options for how it might be treated in the financial statements.

[*Before responding to Jane's request you should read the section on Partnership Changes Requiring Adjustments to Asset Values, paying particular attention to issues relating to goodwill, in Chapter 36, Section 36.5 of* **Connolly**.]

Ethical Dilemma

Your firm holds a practising certificate with audit qualification from Chartered Accountants Ireland. It has joined a network arrangement with other accountants because it promised client support, as well as discounted professional indemnity insurance, group advertising, and full technical backup. Your firm paid a joining fee and pays an annual charge based on turnover. Your firm also has to meet the network's conditions to undertake all work for a fixed fee and be available 24/7. The network advertises as a one-stop shop able to undertake a full range of accounting and auditing services. The director of the network has approach your firm and asked that your firm, for the good of the network, sign off the audit report on a set of accounts prepared by another member of the network who does not hold an audit qualification certificate. He has assured the firm that 'it's only a matter of putting your signature to the report, because the client is well-known to the network'.

Task 15

What should your firm do?

Meeting 3 – 3 January 2014

You have arranged to meet with Maire Louise Phillips to discuss the preparation of the accounts of the Poulenc Partnership for the year ended 31 December 2013. At the meeting, you discover the following information:

On 1 July 2013, Joseph Phillips retired from the partnership and it was agreed that Jane should be admitted as a partner on the same date. Jane paid €/£50,000 into the partnership on 1 July 2013. This amount included €/£9,000 in respect of Jane's share of goodwill. A goodwill account is not to be maintained permanently in the accounts of the partnership. The revised profit-sharing arrangements are:

1. Interest on capital is to be provided at a rate of 10% per annum.
2. Ellen is to receive a salary of €/£10,000 per annum.
3. The balance of profit or loss is to be divided between the partners in the ratio:
    - Maire Louise Phillips – 25%;
    - Christopher Pringle – 20%;
    - Caiti Pollen – 25%;
    - Ellen Peterson – 15%; and
    - Jane Dough – 15%.

On his retirement, Joseph Phillips' partnership account is to be converted into a loan account; although the earliest that Joseph can ask for it to be repaid is 1 January 2014.

Maire Louise Phillips also provided you with the following trial balance for the Poulenc Partnership as at 31 December 2013:

The Poulenc Partnership
Trial Balance
as at 31 December 2013

	Dr €/£	Cr €/£
Sales		750,000
Inventory at 1 January 2013	71,000	
Purchases	400,000	
Trade payables		60,000
Cash at bank	98,000	
Current accounts:		
Maire Louise Phillips		25,250
Joseph Phillips		14,450
Christopher Pringle		25,000
Caiti Pollen		31,750
Ellen Peterson		25,550
Jane Dough		–
Capital accounts:		
Maire Louise Phillips		45,000
Joseph Phillips		40,000
Christopher Pringle		34,000
Caiti Pollen		50,000
Ellen Peterson		26,000
Jane Dough		50,000
Drawings:		
Maire Louise Phillips	40,000	
Joseph Phillips	20,000	
Christopher Pringle	25,000	
Caiti Pollen	34,000	
Ellen Peterson	20,000	
Jane Dough	12,000	
General expenses	40,000	
Trade receivables	170,000	
Premises – cost as at 1 January 2013	80,000	
Premises – accumulated depreciation as at 1 January 2013		14,000
Premises – additions during 2013	140,000	
Fixtures and fittings – cost as at 1 January 2013	24,000	
Fixtures and fittings – accumulated depreciation as at 1 January 2013		10,000
Fixtures and fittings – additions during 2013	27,000	
	1,201,000	1,201,000

16 CA PROFICIENCY I: FINANCIAL ACCOUNTING TOOLKIT

The partners have advised that the following adjustments need to be made to the trial balance:

1. Inventory

An inventory-take was conducted at 31 December 2013. Inventory was valued at €/£90,000 based on cost. However, 15% of this inventory has a net realisable value of only €/£8,500. A further €/£4,000 of the total inventory is considered obsolete and should be written off.

2. Non-current assets

No depreciation for the year ended 31 December 2013 has been included in the draft trial balance. Depreciation should be provided for as follows:

Premises — on a straight-line basis over 40 years; and
Fixtures and fittings — on a straight-line basis over 6 years.

A full year's depreciation is charged in the year of acquisition and none in the year of disposal.

3. Trade receivables

An allowance for recoverable debts of €/£1,000 is to be provided for. General bad debts should be provided for, based on 1.5% of all remaining trade receivables.

4. Accruals

Year-end accruals have not been included in the draft trial balance, and are to be provided for as follows: accountancy €/£2,500; heat and light €/£500; and telephone €/£215.

5. Capital grant

At 31 December 2013, a capital grant of €/£14,000 was receivable from the Tourist Board in respect of the year's property additions. This is to be released to the income statement in line with depreciation. No entries have been included in the draft trial balance in respect of this capital grant.

6. Profits and losses accrue evenly over the year.

7. No revaluation of non-current assets was required at any time during 2013.

Task 16

The partners have requested that you prepare the accounts of the Poulenc Partnership for the year ended 31 December 2013.

*[Before responding to the partners' request you should read the sections on Basic Partnership Changes and Partnership Changes Requiring Adjustments to Asset Values in Chapter 36 of **Connolly**.]*

Meeting 4 – 31 January 2014

After preparing the partnership accounts for the year ended 31 December 2013 you are informed that, on 1 January 2014, the Poulenc Partnership formed a company, Poulenc Company Limited, to take over the assets and liabilities of the partnership on that date. The agreement provides that the non-current assets of the partnership be taken over at the following values:

Premises	€/£250,000
Fixtures and fittings	€/£33,000

All other assets and liabilities are to be taken over at their book values at 31 December 2013.

Poulenc Company Limited is to issue €/£1 ordinary shares to the partners in proportion to the final balances remaining on their capital accounts, after transferring current account balances at 31 December 2013. The partners will become directors in Poulenc Company Limited and each will receive director's fees of €/£10,000 per annum.

Task 17

You have been asked to close off the books of the Poulenc Partnership and prepare an opening statement of financial position for Poulenc Company Limited as at 1 January 2014.

*[Before responding to the partners' request, you should read the sections on Dissolution of a Partnership and Conversion to a Limited Company in Chapter 36 of **Connolly**.]*

Ethical Dilemma

Your firm has recently taken on new clients: a partnership and the tax affairs of the two individual partners who are otherwise unconnected. You have become closely involved in their affairs and, as your firm was completing the partnership accounts, it was informed that one of the partners is intending to leave the partnership. The two partners have agreed the figure to be paid for the goodwill of the business (which is all internally generated and not included in the statement of financial position). It has been further agreed between the two partners that the outgoing partner will be paid the balance on his capital account.

A property, which is owned jointly by the two partners, has been included in the partnership accounts at its written down historic cost of €/£75,000. In preparation for buying out the partner who is leaving, the property has been transferred into the name of the remaining partner, who has taken out a mortgage on the property. For the purposes of the new mortgage, the property has been valued at €/£150,000. The partnership is a very profitable one, and the work will continue to be carried out by the remaining partner who will trade as a sole trader. Her partner had undertaken the administration and bookkeeping for the partnership.

You are uncomfortable about this position as your firm acts as accountant/tax advisor for all three parties and you are also concerned that the partner who is leaving does not appear to be getting anything for his share of the increase in the value of the property.

Task 18

What should you do?

CONCLUSION

Having studied this section on partnership accounts, you should understand the following key points:

- The initial capital put into a partnership by each partner is shown by means of a capital account for each partner.
- Each partner also has a current account.
- The net profit of a partnership is appropriated by the partners according to a previously agreed ratio.
- Partners may be charged interest on their drawings and may receive interest on capital. If a partner makes a loan to the business, he will receive interest on it in the normal manner.
- On admission or retirement of a partner, one partnership ends and another begins. The goodwill of the old partnership must be valued and attributed to the old partners in the old profit-sharing ratio, as should any profit or loss on revaluation of assets. If goodwill (or revaluation profits and losses) are not to be retained in the books of the partnership, they must be attributed to the new partners in the new profit-sharing ratio (debit capital accounts for goodwill and revaluation surplus, credit for revaluation deficit).
- The conversion of a partnership to a limited company effectively involves the dissolution of the partnership. The assets are transferred to the company in exchange for an issue of shares and loan stock.

*[And finally, you should now attempt the Self-test Questions, Review Questions and Challenging Questions at the end of Chapter 36 of **Connolly**.]*

SECTION THREE

LIMITED COMPANY: MY COMPANY LIMITED (MCL)

INTRODUCTION

The form and content of financial statements is addressed in IAS 1 *Presentation of Financial Statements*, the objective of which is to prescribe the basis for presentation of general purpose financial statements, ensure comparability both with the entity's financial statements of previous periods and with the financial statements of other entities. To achieve this objective, IAS 1 sets out overall requirements for the presentation of financial statements, guidelines for their structure and minimum requirements for their content.

In June 2011, the International Accounting Standards Board (IASB) issued amendments to IAS 1 *Presentation of Financial Statements* (see Chapter 2 of *Connolly*). In the main, these amendments affected the title of the performance statement and the presentation of other comprehensive income (OCI) within the statement. Each of these is now addressed in turn.

With respect to the name of the statement, it was proposed that the title 'Statement of Profit or Loss and Other Comprehensive Income' (SPLOCI) be adopted (often referred to previously as an 'income statement', 'profit and loss account' or 'statement of comprehensive income' (SoCI)). While IAS 1 still permits the use of other titles (e.g. SoCI), this Toolkit applies the designation SPLOCI whenever the full statement is being considered, described or referred to in this section, Section Three, and Section Four, which deal with the preparation of company and consolidated financial statements respectively.

In broad terms, regardless of the title adopted, the statement is divided into two components: a statement of profit or loss, and OCI. The former section shows the revenues from operations, expenses of operating and the resulting net profit or loss over a specific period of time; while OCI includes items such as changes in revaluation surplus, actuarial gains and losses on defined benefit plans recognised in accordance with IAS 19 *Employee Benefits* (see Chapter 17 of *Connolly*) and gains and losses arising from translating the financial statements of a foreign operation (IAS 21 *The Effects of Changes in Foreign Exchange Rates* – see Chapter 31 of *Connolly*). Reporting entities have the option of presenting profit or loss and OCI either in a single continuous statement or in two separate, but consecutive, statements. For clarity (e.g. with respect to journal entries), this text distinguishes between the two components as follows: Statement of Profit or Loss and Other Comprehensive Income – Profit or Loss (SPLOCI – P/L); and Statement of Profit or Loss and Other Comprehensive Income – Other Comprehensive Income (SPLOCI – OCI).

Regarding the presentation of OCI, the changes were driven by a desire to address a perceived lack of distinction between different items in OCI, as well as a lack of clarity in the presentation of those items. For example, while some items in OCI could have a considerable effect on the financial performance of an entity if they were to be recycled through profit or loss, this impact was unclear based upon the presentation requirements prior to the amendments. In addition, while previously only a limited number of transactions were recognised in OCI, changes to IFRSs (e.g. IAS 19 and IFRS 9 *Financial Instruments* – see Chapter 25 of *Connolly*) have led to increased recognition of items within OCI. As a result, the amendments to IAS 1 change the grouping of items presented in OCI, with items that could be reclassified (or 'recycled') to profit or loss at a future point in time (e.g. upon de-recognition or settlement) being presented separately from items which will never be reclassified.

Examples of OCI items that can be reclassified into profit or loss include:

- foreign exchange gains and losses arising from translations of financial statements of a foreign operation (on the disposal of a foreign operation) (IAS 21); and
- effective portion of gains and losses on hedging instruments in a cash flow hedge (IAS 39 *Financial Instruments: Recognition and Measurement* – see Chapter 25 of *Connolly*).

Examples of OCI items that cannot be reclassified into profit or loss include:

- changes in revaluation surplus (IAS 16 *Property, Plant and Equipment* – see Chapter 6 of *Connolly* and IAS 38 *Intangible Assets* – see Chapter 9 of *Connolly*);
- actuarial gains and losses on defined benefit plans (IAS 19);
- gains and losses from investments in equity instruments measured at fair value through OCI (IFRS 9); and
- for those liabilities designated at fair value through profit or loss, changes in fair value attributable to changes in the liability's credit risk (IFRS 9).

Figure 3.1 below illustrates the Statement of OCI after the IAS 1 amendments relating to OCI have been applied.

Figure 3.1: Statement of OCI after the IAS 1 Amendments are Applied

Other Comprehensive Income	2012 €000	2011 €000
Items that may be reclassified into profit or loss		
Foreign exchange gains arising from the translation of foreign operations	1,771	1,071
Share of associate's OCI	–	412

Change in value of the effective portion of derivatives designated in qualifying cash flow hedges	73	601
Tax related to OCI items that may be reclassified to profit or loss	(189)	(715)
	1,655	1,369

Items that will not be reclassified into profit or loss

Revaluation of property, plant and equipment	4,460	(1,154)
Remeasurement of net defined benefit liability	266	157
(Loss)/gain from investments in equity instruments measured at fair value through OCI	(358)	1,542
Fair value through profit or loss - changes in fair value attributable to changes in the liability's credit risk	4	(15)
Tax related to OCI items that will not be reclassified to profit or loss	(1,175)	279
	3,197	809
Total other comprehensive income	4,852	2,178

The amendments to OCI do not change the nature of the items that are recognised in OCI, nor do they impact the determination as to whether items in OCI are reclassified through profit or loss in future periods. Furthermore, entities are still permitted to present components of OCI either net of the related tax effects or before tax with one amount shown for the aggregate amount of income tax relating to those components. However, if an entity presents OCI items before the related tax effects, then tax is required to be allocated and disclosed separately for each of the two OCI groups (i.e. the total amount of tax is required to be split into two amounts, being tax related to items that might be reclassified subsequently to profit or loss and tax relating to those items that will not be reclassified subsequently to profit or loss).

While the change in presentation of OCI is relatively minor with respect to the overall financial statements, it should allow financial statement users to more easily identify the potential impact that OCI items may have on future profit or loss. Although the IASB acknowledges that the amendments did not address the issue of the lack of clear underlying principles for the recognition of OCI items (as well as for the reclassification of such items to profit or loss) within IFRSs, it accepts that further work is needed to develop a clear principle for measuring performance items such as OCI. This is likely to take considerable time to develop.

The amendments to IAS 1 are effective for annual periods beginning on or after 1 July 2012, with early adoption permitted. If an entity applies the amendments for an earlier period it is required to disclose that fact. It is important to remember that reporting entities continue to have the option of presenting profit or loss and OCI either in a single continuous statement or in two separate, but consecutive, statements.

(*Note*: IAS 1 is applied, in Section Three, and Section Four, which deal with the preparation of company and consolidated financial statements respectively. Given the nature of sole trader (Section One) and partnership (Section Two) accounts, it was considered more appropriate to use the terms 'income statement' and 'cash flow statement' in these sections; however, the term 'statement of financial position' is applied throughout the text (rather than 'balance sheet'). It was not considered necessary to apply strictly IAS 1 formats for the three financial statements in Section One and Section Two.)

By the end of Section Three, with respect to the financial accounting aspects of the course, you should be able to:

- understand the generally accepted accounting principles underlying the preparation of financial statements;
- explain the purpose of financial reporting;
- describe the accounting principles as contained in the *Conceptual Framework for Financial Reporting 2010 (IFRS Framework)* document;
- prepare and present the primary financial statements in accordance with international accounting standards; and
- format notes to the financial statements.

[Before attempting this section, you may find it useful to read Chapter 2: Presentation of Financial Statements in your core textbook International Financial Accounting and Reporting (4th Edition) *by Ciaran Connolly ('**Connolly**'), and complete the Self-test Questions, Review Questions and Challenging Questions at the end of that chapter.]*

COFFEE TIME

Each week while on secondment at MCL, Mike always tries to find time for a coffee and a chat. However, after discussing the back pages and other recent events, Mike tends to ask for your opinion on various accounting issues.

Task 19

Prepare a response to each of the **following** issues raised by Mike.

Coffee – 31 January 2012

I used to believe that revenue recognition was very straightforward, but recently as MCL's business has become more complex, I'm not so sure. What are the broad approaches to revenue recognition?

*[Before responding to Mike's question, you should read Chapter 4: Revenue Recognition in **Connolly**, and then attempt the Self-test Questions, Review Questions and Challenging Questions at the end of that chapter.]*

Coffee – 14 February 2012

What might be some of the reasons why the European Union decided to require all listed companies to prepare their consolidated financial statements in conformity with IASs/IFRSs?

*[Before responding to Mike's question you should read the section on the Regulatory Framework in Chapter 1: Framework for Financial Reporting of **Connolly**.]*

Coffee – 17 March 2012

Applying the *IFRS Framework* document is subjective and requires judgement. Would the IASB be better off abandoning the *IFRS Framework* and, instead, rely on a very active interpretations committee that develops detailed guidance in response to requests from constituents?

*[Before responding to Mike's question you should read the section on the Conceptual Framework for Financial Reporting in Chapter 1 of **Connolly**.]*

Coffee – 11 April 2012

When I studied accounting, we were taught always to be conservative in recognition or measurement. When in doubt, the rule was don't put the asset on the statement of financial position, or if it's there, write it down at the first sign of trouble and never recognise profit until a sale takes place. Does the *IFRS Framework* document support this approach?

*[Before responding to Mike's question you should read the section on the Conceptual Framework for Financial Reporting in Chapter 1 of **Connolly**.]*

Coffee – 30 April 2012

What is meant when people say that accounting information should be 'decision-useful'?

*[Before responding to Mike's question you should read the section on the Conceptual Framework for Financial Reporting in Chapter 1 of **Connolly**.]*

Coffee – 20 May 2012

How does accounting profit and taxable profit differ and how is each treated when accounting for income taxes?

*[Before responding to Mike's question you will find it useful to read the sections on Current Tax and Deferred Tax in Chapter 13 of **Connolly**.]*

Coffee – 14 June 2012

What action should be taken when a tax rate or tax rule changes, and why?

*[Before responding to Mike's question you may find it useful to read the section on Current Tax in Chapter 13 of **Connolly**.]*

Coffee – 14 July 2012

What is the objective of a statement of financial position and what are the major limitations of a statement of financial position as a source of information for general users of financial statements?

*[Before responding to Mike's question you should read the section on the Conceptual Framework for Financial Reporting in Chapter 1 of **Connolly**.]*

Coffee – 4 August 2012

Expenses are required to be classified either on the face of the statement of profit or loss and other comprehensive income or in the notes according to their nature or function, whichever provides the more relevant and reliable information. But what is meant by classification by nature or function? Which basis might ordinarily provide more relevant and reliable information to users of financial information?

*[Before responding to Mike's question you should read Chapter 2: Presentation of Financial Statements of **Connolly**.]*

Coffee – 3 September 2012

What is the benefit of including details of accounting policies in the notes to the accounts?

*[Before responding to Mike's question you should read the section on the Structure and Content of Financial Statements in Chapter 2 of **Connolly**.]*

Coffee – 10 October 2012

How should each of the following items be classified in the statement of financial position:

Trade receivables; Work-in-progress; Trade payables; Prepayments; Property; Goodwill; Debentures outstanding; Preference share capital; Unearned revenue; Accrued salaries; Trading securities held; Share capital; and Dividends payable?

*[Before responding to Mike's question you should read Chapter 2 and then complete the Self-test Questions, Review Questions and Challenging Questions at the end of **Connolly**.]*

Coffee – 1 November 2012

The introduction of international accounting standards has received considerable publicity. What do you think are the key practical changes to be aware of?

Ethical Dilemma

The senior audit partner in your firm is about to retire. One of your firm's long-standing audit clients has asked him to become a non-executive director at a nominal salary and this is a role he would like to accept. However, he is concerned because the firm is not in a position to repay his capital account in one lump sum (currently standing at €/£180,000) and it has been informally agreed that he will be paid in equal instalments at quarterly intervals over the next three years. No agreement to this effect has yet been signed because there are other issues still to be determined.

What should the retiring partner do?

Coffee – 28 November 2012

I know that a set of financial statements includes a statement of financial position, a statement of profit or loss and other comprehensive income, a statement of cash flows and accounting policies and explanatory notes. However, while I have a reasonable grasp of these different elements, I must admit that the statement of changes in equity is a mystery to me.

*[Before responding to Mike's question you should read the section on the Structure and Content of Financial Statements in Chapter 2 of **Connolly**.]*

MY COMPANY LIMITED
PREPARATION OF FINANCIAL STATEMENTS
For The Year Ended 31 December 2012

The following comprehensive example addresses a number of the specific CAP 1 financial accounting functional competencies. While the example deals with a wide range of issues, you must understand the material covered in the following chapters of *Connolly* before attempting it: Chapter 2: Presentation of Financial Statement; Chapter 11: Inventories; and Chapter 19: Statement of Cash Flows – Single Company.

A skeletal accounts file has been prepared as a template for your solutions. Under the guidance of your lecturer, you should follow the instructions given below in order to complete the file. The suggested solutions present the 'answers' as a completed accounts file.

Instructions/Guidance

1. Begin with:
   - draft TB (Section E);
   - draft statement of profit or loss and other comprehensive income lead schedule (Section F);
   - draft statement of financial position lead schedules and supporting notes (Section G); and
   - end of year adjustments (Section D).

Exercise

Using the draft TB (Section E), prepare 'lead schedules' for each of the statement of financial position headings, and then compare with the draft statement of financial position lead schedules in Section G.

2. Then:
   - calculate end of year adjustments (Section D), and check answers and adjusting journals (Section C).
3. Then:
   - complete 'blank' final TB (Section B);
   - update draft statement of profit or loss and other comprehensive income lead schedule (Section F); and
   - update draft statement of financial position lead schedules (Section G).
4. Then:
   - compare with final/completed TB (Section B);
   - compare with final/completed statement of profit or loss and other comprehensive income lead schedule (Section F); and

- compare with final/completed statement of financial position lead schedules (Section G).

(The final/completed schedules, together with the notes to the financial statements, are included in the Suggested Solutions section below.)

5. Then
    - complete draft statement of cash flows schedule (Section H); and
    - compare with final/completed statement of cash flows schedule (Section H).

6. Then:
    - complete 'blank' statement of profit or loss and other comprehensive income, statement of financial position, statement of cash flows and statement of changes in equity (Section A);
    - compare with final/completed versions (Section A); and
    - review notes to the financial statements (Section A), discuss and cross-reference.

Learning Objectives

Having studied this section on the preparation of company financial statements, you should understand the following key points:

- the generally accepted accounting principles underlying the preparation of company financial statements;
- the purpose of corporate financial reporting;
- the accounting principles as contained in the *IFRS Framework* document; and
- how to prepare and present the primary financial statements, together with the relevant disclosure notes, in accordance with international accounting standards.

CONTENTS

Section

A. Financial Statements
B. Final Trial Balance
C. Adjusting Journal Entries
D. End of Year Adjustments
E. Draft Trial Balance
F. Statement of Profit or Loss and Other Comprehensive Income Lead Schedule
G. Statement of Financial Position Lead Schedules
H. Statement of Cash Flows Lead Schedule

SECTION A: FINANCIAL STATEMENTS

My Company Limited
STATEMENT OF PROFIT OR LOSS AND OTHER COMPREHENSIVE INCOME
Year ended 31 December 2012

	Note	31 December 2012 €/£	31 December 2012 €/£	31 December 2011 €/£	31 December 2011 €/£
Revenue					1,310,300
Cost of Sales:					
Opening inventory				60,000	
Purchases				396,200	
Closing inventory				(77,800)	
				378,400	
Manufacturing staff costs				383,100	
Depreciation plant and machinery				22,600	
Loss on disposal of equipment				–	(784,100)
Gross Profit					526,200
Distribution Costs:					
Staff costs				256,300	
Depreciation fixtures and fittings				19,780	(276,080)
Administrative Expenses:					
Staff costs				20,000	
Depreciation freehold properties				8,400	
Amortisation software licences				10,000	
Other				117,400	(155,800)
Operating Profit					94,320
Finance cost					(37,610)
Profit before tax					56,710
Income tax expense					(11,000)
Profit after tax					45,710
Other comprehensive income					–
Total comprehensive income					45,710

My Company Limited
STATEMENT OF FINANCIAL POSITION
31 December 2012

	Note	31 December 2012 €/£	31 December 2012 €/£	31 December 2011 €/£	31 December 2011 €/£
ASSETS					
Non-current Assets					
Freehold properties					219,859
Plant and equipment					132,745
Fixtures and fittings					48,521
					401,125
Intangible – software licences					60,000
					461,125
Current Assets					
Inventory – Raw materials			40,200		
– Work in progress			18,100		
– Finished goods			19,500		
Trade receivables			95,950		
Other receivables			2,700		
Prepayments			1,400		
Bank and cash			10,254		188,104
					649,229
EQUITY AND LIABILITIES					
Capital and Reserves					
€/£1 ordinary shares					100,000
Revaluation reserve					24,525
Retained earnings					364,914
					489,439
Non-current Liabilities					
Provision for liabilities and charges					35,000
Current Liabilities					
Trade payables			19,473		
Other payables			103,417		
Accruals			1,900		124,790
					649,229

My Company Limited
Cash Flow Statement
Year ended 31 December 2012

	Note	31 December 2012 €/£	31 December 2011 €/£
Net cash flow from operating activities			183,461
Cash flows from investing activities			(187,961)
Cash flows from financing activities			5,000
Net increase in cash and cash equivalents			500
Cash and cash equivalents at start of year			9,754
Cash and cash equivalents at end of year			10,254

My Company Limited
Statement of Changes in Equity
Year ended 31 December 2012

	Share capital €/£	Revaluation reserve €/£	Retained earnings €/£	Total €/£
At 1 January 2012	100,000	24,525	364,914	489,439
Changes in equity for the year: Recognised in total comprehensive income				
At 31 December 2012				

SECTION B: FINAL TRIAL BALANCE

My Company Limited
Final Trial Balance
31 December 2012

	€/£ DR	€/£ CR
Purchases of materials		
Manufacturing staff costs:		
Salaries and wages		
Social security costs		
Other pension costs		
Administrative costs:		
Telephone		
Heat and light		
Insurance		
Hire of plant and machinery		
Audit		
Staff training and development		
Irrecoverable debts		
General		
Depreciation		
Amortisation		
Sales		
Profit/loss on disposal of equipment		
Finance charges		
Administrative staff costs:		
Salaries and wages		
Social security costs		
Other pension costs		
Distribution staff costs:		
Salaries and wages		
Social security costs		
Other pension costs		
Income tax		
Intangible non-current assets:		
Software licences – Cost at 1.1.12		
Software licences – Amortisation at 1.1.12		
– Amortisation charge		

	€/£ DR	€/£ CR

Property, Plant and Equipment, and Fixtures and Fittings:
   Freehold properties   – Cost/valuation at 1.1.12
                            – Additions
                            – Revaluation
   Freehold properties   – Depreciation at 1.1.12
                            – Charge for year
   Plant and equipment – Cost at 1.1.12
                            – Additions
                            – Disposals
   Plant and equipment – Depreciation at 1.1.12
                            – On disposals
                            – Charge for year
   Fixtures and fittings   – Cost at 1.1.12
                            – Additions
   Fixtures and fittings   – Depreciation at 1.1.12
                            – Charge for year

Inventory:
   Raw materials
   Work-in-progress
   Finished goods

Receivables:
   Trade
   Allowance for irrecoverable debts
   Other receivables
   Prepayments

Cash at bank
Cash-in-hand

Current liabilities:
   Trade payables
   Other payables
   Accruals

Provision for liabilities and charges:
   Early retirement and pension costs

Revaluation reserve – freehold properties
€/£1 ordinary shares
Retained earnings

SECTION C: ADJUSTING JOURNAL ENTRIES

My Company Limited
Adjusting Journal Entries (AJE)
Year ended 31 December 2012

	€/£ DR	€/£ CR

SECTION D: END OF YEAR ADJUSTMENTS

My Company Limited
END OF YEAR ADJUSTMENTS
31 December 2012

1. The trial balance shows a debit balance of €/£10,323 at 31 December 2012, whereas the bank statement indicates that MCL is overdrawn by €/£590.

   Following an examination of MCL's records and the bank statement for the period since the last reconciliation, a number of items were noted:

   (a) A standing order for electricity of €/£10,300 had been paid by the bank on 24 December 2012 but no entry had been made in the cash book.
   (b) A credit transfer of €/£10,200 had been received by the bank on 28 December 2012 in settlement of one of MCL's customer accounts. No entry had been made for this in the cash book.
   (c) Cheques from customers totalling €/£11,054 were entered in the cash book on 31 December 2012 but did not clear the bank until 1 January 2013.
   (d) Cheques issued by MCL to pay trade payables on 29 December 2012 totalling €/£241 did not appear on the bank statement until February 2013.

2. Amortisation of software licences for year ended 31 December 2012 has not yet been provided.

3. After inventory taking for the year ended 31 December 2012 had taken place, the closing inventory of MCL was valued as follows:

	€/£
Raw materials	44,500
Work-in-progress	19,000
Finished goods	21,500
	85,000

   Following a detailed review of the inventory-take working papers and discussions with staff, the facts noted below were discovered.

   (a) Some finished goods stored outside had been included at their normal cost price of €/£5,700. They had, however, deteriorated and would require an estimated €/£1,200 to be spent to restore them to their original condition, after which they could be sold for €/£8,000.
   (b) Some raw materials had been damaged and were now unusable. They could, however, be sold for €/£1,100 as spares after repairs estimated at €/£400 had been carried out. They had originally cost €/£2,000.
   (c) One inventory sheet used to record raw materials had been over-added by €/£1,260 and another recording finished goods under-added by €/£720.
   (d) MCL has received raw materials costing €/£4,010 during the last week of December 2012 but, because the invoices did not arrive until February 2013, they have not been included in inventory.

(e) An inventory sheet total of €/£12,340 for work-in-progress has been transferred to a summary sheet as €/£14,230.

(f) Invoices totalling €/£16,380 arrived during the last week of December 2012 (and were included in purchases and payables) but, because of transport delays, the goods did not arrive until late February 2013 and were not included in closing inventory.

(g) Portable generators on hire from another company at a charge of €/£3,470 were included, at this figure, in the inventory of finished goods.

(h) Free samples sent to MCL by various suppliers had been included in the raw materials inventory at the catalogue price of €/£2,425.

(i) Goods costing €/£4,180 sent to customers on a sale or return basis had been included in raw materials inventory by MCL at their selling price of €/£6,020.

(j) Goods sent on a sale or return basis to MCL had been included in the raw materials inventory at the amount payable (€/£2,670) if retained. No decision to retain these items had been made.

4. It is company policy to maintain the allowance for irrecoverable debts at an amount which is equal to 5% of trade receivables at the reporting date.

5. MCL leases certain plant and machinery and pays for them in advance each quarter. During the year ended 31 December 2012, MCL made the following payments in respect of the plant and machinery:

Date Paid	Amount	For Quarter Ending
1.11.11	€/£4,200	31.1.12
1.2.12	€/£4,300	30.4.12
1.5.12	€/£4,400	31.7.12
1.8.12	€/£4,400	31.10.12
1.11.12	€/£4,500	31.1.13

All payments made in year ended 31 December 2012 have been charged in full to the statement of profit or loss and other comprehensive income – profit or loss.

6. The balance on the Trade Payables Account at 31 December 2012 was €/£15,033.

The balances on the individual accounts in the Payables Ledger were extracted and totalled €/£9,333.

A detailed review of the information highlighted the following:

(a) a credit balance of €/£3,400 had been omitted from the list of balances;

(b) no entry had been made to Mr Can's individual ledger account in respect of an invoice for €/£2,300 which was correctly recorded in the Purchases Day Book;

(c) an invoice from Mr Able for €/£7,000 had not been recorded in the Purchases Day Book;

(d) an invoice from Mr Will for €/£1,500 had been recorded twice in error in the Purchases Day Book.

7. MCL receives its telephone bills quarterly just after the end of each quarter has elapsed. It received the following bills during the last year which it paid on the dates shown.

For Telephone From To	Amount €/£	Date bill received	Date bill paid
1 Oct 2011 – 31 Dec 2011	1,900	10 Jan 2012	29 Jan 2012
1 Jan 2012 – 31 Mar 2012	1,800	10 Apr 2012	1 May 2012
1 Apr 2012 – 30 Jun 2012	1,600	9 Jul 2012	31 Jul 2012
1 Jul 2012 – 30 Sept 2012	2,200	12 Oct 2012	1 Nov 2012
1 Oct 2012 – 31 Dec 2012	2,000	13 Jan 2013	2 Feb 2013

   All payments made during year ended 31 December 2012 have been charged to the statement of profit or loss and other comprehensive income in arriving at profit or loss.

8. Depreciation of property, plant and equipment, and fixtures and fittings for the year ended 31 December 2012 has not yet been provided for in the financial statements.

9. MCL's tax charge for 2012, which takes into account all relevant items, is €/£50,000.

SECTION E: DRAFT TRIAL BALANCE

My Company Limited
Draft Trial Balance
31 December 2012

	€/£ DR	€/£ CR
Purchases of materials	423,800	
Manufacturing staff costs:		
Salaries and wages	310,250	
Social security costs	40,800	
Other pension costs	69,200	
Administrative costs:		
Telephone	7,500	
Heat and light	31,450	
Insurance	15,200	
Hire of plant and machinery	17,600	
Audit	24,100	
Staff training and development	13,300	
General	9,300	
Sales		1,637,600
Profit/loss on disposal of equipment	2,000	
Finance charges	36,829	
Administrative staff costs:		
Salaries and wages	26,500	
Social security costs	3,500	
Other pension costs	4,100	
Distribution staff costs:		
Salaries and wages	239,000	
Social security costs	44,000	
Other pension costs	7,000	
Intangible non-current assets:		
Software licences – Cost at 1.1.12	80,000	
Software licences – Amortisation at 1.1.12		20,000
Property, plant and equipment, and fixtures and fittings:		
Freehold properties – Cost/valuation at 1.1.12	420,000	
– Additions	200,000	
– Revaluation	21,000	
Freehold properties – Depreciation at 1.1.12		200,141
Plant and equipment – Cost at 1.1.12	226,000	
– Additions	15,000	
– Disposals		10,000
Plant and equipment – Depreciation at 1.1.12		93,255
– On disposals	6,000	

	€/£ DR	€/£ CR
Fixtures and fittings — Cost at 1.1.12	98,900	
— Additions	4,000	
Fixtures and fittings — Depreciation at 1.1.12		50,379
Inventory:		
Raw materials	44,500	
Work-in-progress	19,000	
Finished goods	21,500	
Receivables:		
Trade	115,400	
Allowance for irrecoverable debts		5,050
Other receivables	3,400	
Prepayments (hire of plant and machinery)		1,400
Cash at bank	10,323	
Cash-in-hand	100	
Current liabilities:		
Trade payables		15,033
Other payables (current tax)		4,700
Accruals (telephone)		1,900
Provision for liabilities and charges:		
Early retirement and pension costs		50,000
Revaluation reserve – freehold properties		45,525
€/£1 ordinary shares		100,000
Retained earnings		378,369
	2,611,952	2,611,952

SECTION F: STATEMENT OF PROFIT OR LOSS AND OTHER COMPREHENSIVE INCOME

My Company Limited
STATEMENT OF PROFIT OR LOSS AND OTHER COMPREHENSIVE INCOME
Year ended 31 December 2012

	2012 €/£	2011 €/£
Revenue		1,310,300
Cost of Sales		
Opening inventory		60,000
Purchases		396,200
Closing inventory		(77,800)
		378,400
Manufacturing staff costs		383,100
Depreciation plant and machinery		22,600
Loss on disposal of equipment		-
		784,100
Distribution Costs		
Staff costs		256,300
Depreciation fixtures and fittings		19,780
		276,080
Administrative Expenses		
Staff costs		20,000
Depreciation freehold properties		8,400
Amortisation software licences		10,000
Other		117,400
		155,800
Finance cost		37,610
Income tax expense		11,000

SECTION G: STATEMENT OF FINANCIAL POSITION

My Company Limited
INTANGIBLE NON-CURRENT ASSETS
Year ended 31 December 2012

Software Licences	€/£
Cost/Valuation:	
At 1.1.12	80,000
Additions	-
Disposals	-
At 31.12.12	80,000
Amortisation:	
At 1.1.12	20,000
Provided during year	
At 31.12.12	
Net Book Value:	
At 31.12.12	
At 31.12.11	60,000

Notes

1. Intangible non-current assets comprise the value of capitalised operational software licences. The value of licences is amortised on a straight-line basis over their expected useful lives of 8 years.
2. It is company policy to charge the amortisation of software licences to administrative expenses.
3. A valuation of these licences was undertaken by AA Consultants on 1 January 2012.

My Company Limited
Property, Plant and Equipment and Fixtures and Fittings
Year ended 31 December 2012

	Freehold Properties €/£	Plant and Equipment €/£	Fixtures and Fittings €/£	Total €/£
Cost/Valuation:				
At 1 January 2012	420,000	226,000	98,900	744,900
Additions	200,000	15,000	4,000	219,000
Disposals	–	(10,000)	–	(10,000)
Revaluation	21,000	–	–	21,000
At 31 December 2012	641,000	231,000	102,900	974,900
Depreciation:				
At 1 January 2012	200,141	93,255	50,379	343,775
Charged in year				
On disposals	–	(6,000)	–	(6,000)
At 31 December 2012				
Net Book Value:				
At 31 December 2012				
At 31 December 2011	219,859	132,745	48,521	401,125

Notes

1. My Company Limited holds the title to all freehold properties recorded on the statement of financial position. Such properties have been included on the basis of professional valuations. Freehold properties were revalued on 31 December 2012 by Anybody, Chartered Surveyors, on the basis of open market value for existing use.

2. The minimum level for capitalisation of an item of property, plant and equipment, and fixtures and fittings is €/£500.

3. Depreciation is provided at rates calculated to write off the valuation of freehold properties, plant and equipment, and fixtures and fittings by equal instalments over their estimated useful lives as follows:

   Freehold properties – 50 years

   Plant and equipment – 10 years

   Fixtures and fittings – 5 years.

   A full year's depreciation is charged in year of acquisition and none in the year of disposal.

   It is company policy to charge depreciation as follows:

   Freehold properties – administration expenses

   Plant and equipment – cost of sales

   Fixtures and fittings – distribution costs.

4. During the year ended 31 December 2012, equipment with an original cost of €/£10,000 (accumulated depreciation €/£6,000) was sold for €/£2,000 cash.

My Company Limited
Inventory and Work in Progress
Year ended 31 December 2012

	Draft TB €/£	Adjustments DR €/£	(CR) €/£	31 December 2012 €/£	31 December 2011 €/£
Raw materials	44,500				40,200
Work-in-progress	19,000				18,100
Finished goods	21,500				19,500
	85,000				77,800

Notes

1. Inventory and work-in-progress are valued as follows:
   (a) raw materials and finished goods are valued at the lower of cost and net realisable value;
   (b) work-in-progress is valued at the lower of cost, including appropriate overheads, and net realisable value.

2. Inventory valuation is based on accounting custom, and not on the facts of exactly which units are still in inventory at year end. The three main methods of doing this are:
   (a) first in, first out (FIFO)
   (b) last in, first out (LIFO)
   (c) average cost method (AVCO)

   Each of the methods will give a different inventory valuation, and therefore a different profit figure.

3. The net realisable value (NRV) of inventory is calculated as: saleable value less expenses needed before completion of sale. The concept of prudence is used when inventory is valued. Inventory should not be over-valued as otherwise profits will be too high. Therefore, if the net realisable value of inventory is less than the cost of the inventory, the figure to be taken for the final accounts is that of NRV.

4. As closing inventory (before adjustments) at 31 December 2012 is shown in the draft trial balance, the 'retained earnings' in the trial balance will reflect the movement between opening and closing inventory.

My Company Limited
Receivables
Year ended 31 December 2012

	Draft TB €/£	Adjustments DR €/£	Adjustments (CR) €/£	31 December 2012 €/£	31 December 2011 €/£
Trade receivables	115,400				101,000
Allowance for irrecoverable debts	(5,050)				(5,050)
	110,350				95,950
Other receivables – VAT	3,400				2,700
Prepayments – leases	1,400				1,400
	115,150				100,050

My Company Limited
Bank and Cash
Year ended 31 December 2012

	Draft TB €/£	Adjustments DR €/£	Adjustments (CR) €/£	31 December 2012 €/£	31 December 2011 €/£
Bank – no. 1 account	10,323				10,154
Cash-in-hand	100				100
	10,423				10,254

My Company Limited
Payables and Accruals
Year ended 31 December 2012

	Draft TB €/£	Adjustments DR €/£	Adjustments (CR) €/£	31 December 2012 €/£	31 December 2011 €/£
Trade payables	15,033				19,473
Other payables (Income tax)	4,700				103,417
Accruals	1,900				1,900
	21,633				124,790

My Company Limited
Provision for Liabilities and Charges
Year ended 31 December 2012

	Early retirement and pension costs €/£
Balance at 1 January 2012	35,000
Provision during year	15,000
Balance at 31 December 2012	50,000

My Company Limited
Revaluation Reserve
Year ended 31 December 2012

Freehold properties	€/£
Balance at 1 January 2012	24,525
Arising during the year	21,000
Balance at 31 December 2012	45,525

My Company Limited
Retained Earnings
Year ended 31 December 2012

	€/£
Balance at 1 January 2012	364,914
Profit/(loss) for year	
Balance at 31 December 2012	

Note

As closing inventory (before adjustments) at 31 December 2012 is shown in the draft trial balance, the 'retained earnings' in the trial balance reflects the movement between opening and closing inventory.

	€/£
Retained earnings per trial balance	378,369
Inventory at 31 December 2011	77,800
Inventory at 31 December 2012	(91,255)
Therefore retained earnings at 1 January 2012	364,914

SECTION H: STATEMENT OF CASH FLOWS

My Company Limited
STATEMENT OF CASH FLOWS
Year ended 31 December 2012

WORKINGS

2012
€/£

Net cash flow from operating activities
Profit before tax
Depreciation
Amortisation
Interest charge
Loss on disposal
Increase in inventory
Increase in trade receivables
Increase in other receivables
Increase in prepayments
Increase in trade payables
Increase in accruals
Increase in provisions
Interest paid
Tax paid*

Cash flows from investing activities
Purchase of non-current assets
Proceeds from disposal of equipment

* Tax paid
Opening balance
Statement of profit or loss and other comprehensive income
Closing balance

SECTION FOUR

GROUP: THE POT LIMITED GROUP (POT LTD)

INTRODUCTION

In this Toolkit we have previously addressed the fundamental principles and practices of preparing financial statements for:

- Sole Traders (Section One).
- Partnerships (Section Two).
- Limited companies (Section Three).

This section will focus on the preparation of statements of financial position for groups of companies formally known as 'consolidated statements of financial position'.

A group is formed when a parent (P Ltd) acquires a subsidiary (S Ltd) which is achieved by the parent gaining control over that subsidiary. Control over a subsidiary is *de facto* when the parent owns more than 50% of the voting power of the subsidiary and is manifested when the parent has the power to govern the financial and operating policies of the subsidiary so as to obtain benefits from its activities. Both the parent and subsidiary (which are separate entities) continue to prepare their individual financial statements. The statement of financial position of the parent will show a non-current asset entitled 'Investment in S Ltd', which reflects the cost of acquiring a controlling interest in the share capital of that entity.

If you were a shareholder of P Ltd and you received your annual financial statements which included an asset 'Investment in S Ltd' (e.g. a 75% holding) valued at say €350,000, would you be satisfied that this amount of information gives sufficient detail about the assets, liabilities, income, expenses and cash flows of the subsidiary? The answer would be 'No' and this is precisely the reasoning behind consolidated financial statements.

Recent changes and revisions in IASs and IFRSs have affected the suite of IAS/IFRSs dealing with consolidated financial statements. In May 2011, the IASB:

- amended IAS 27 *Consolidated and Separate Financial Statements*, and replaced it with IAS 27 *Separate Financial Statements*;

- amended IAS 28 *Investments in Associates*, and replaced it with IAS 28 *Investments in Associates and Joint Ventures*;
- issued IFRS 10 *Consolidated Financial Statements*;
- issued IFRS 11 *Joint Arrangements*; and
- issued IFRS 12 *Disclosure of Interests in Other Entities*.

All of the above new or amended standards apply to annual reporting periods beginning on or after 1 January 2013, with early application permitted.

Consequently, with respect to consolidated financial statements, the key accounting standards are:

- IAS 27 *Separate Financial Statements* (2011) (discussed in Chapter 26 of **Connolly**);
- IAS 28 *Investments in Associates and Joint Ventures* (discussed in Chapter 29 of **Connolly**);
- IFRS 3 *Business Combinations* (discussed in Chapter 26 of **Connolly**);
- IFRS 10 *Consolidated Financial Statements* (discussed in Chapter 26 of **Connolly**);
- IFRS 11 *Joint Arrangements* (discussed in Chapter 30 of **Connolly**); and
- IFRS 12 *Disclosure of Interests in Other Entities* (discussed in Chapter 26 of **Connolly**).

With respect to the preparation of a consolidated statement of financial position, the two main accounting standards are IFRS 3 and IFRS 10. The key issues with respect to these standards are outlined briefly below.

IFRS 3 *Business Combinations*

IFRS 3 deals with accounting for business combinations and the ongoing accounting for goodwill acquired in business combinations. A business combination is a transaction or event in which an acquirer obtains control of one or more businesses. As noted above, control is the power to govern the financial and operating policies of an entity in order to obtain benefits. Normally this requires more than 50% of an entity's voting rights; this is explained further below in relation to IFRS 10.

All business combinations should be accounted for under the acquisition method. This method recognises that the acquirer acquires the net assets and that the measurement of the acquirer's own net assets are not affected by the transaction. IFRS 3 has an explicit option, available on a transaction-by-transaction basis, to measure any non-controlling interest in the entity acquired either at fair value (new method) or at the non-controlling interest's proportionate share of the net identifiable assets of the entity acquired (old method). For the purpose of measuring non-controlling interest at fair value, it may be possible to determine the acquisition-date fair value on the basis of market prices for the equity shares not held by the acquirer. When a market price for the equity shares is not available because the shares are not publicly traded, the acquirer must measure the fair value of the non-controlling interest using other valuation techniques.

IFRS 10 *Consolidated Financial Statements*

IFRS 10 provides a single consolidation model that identifies control as the basis for consolidation for all types of entities. It:

- requires a parent entity (i.e. an entity that controls one or more other entities) to present consolidated financial statements;
- defines the principle of control, and establishes control as the basis for consolidation;
- sets out how to apply the principle of control to identify whether an investor controls an investee and therefore must consolidate the investee; and
- sets out the accounting requirements for the preparation of consolidated financial statements.

IFRS 10 states that an investor controls an investee if and only if the investor has *all* of the following elements:

- power over the investee – this arises from rights, and such rights can be straightforward (e.g. through voting rights) or complex (e.g. embedded in contractual arrangements);
- exposure, or rights, to variable returns from its involvement with the investee – such returns must have the potential to vary as a result of the investee's performance and can be positive, negative, or both; and
- the ability to use its power over the investee to affect the amount of the investor's returns.

If an investor controls an investee, it is required to prepare consolidated financial statements, *except* if it meets *all* of the following conditions:

- it is a wholly-owned subsidiary or is a partially-owned subsidiary of another entity and its other owners, including those not otherwise entitled to vote, have been informed about, and do not object to, the parent not presenting consolidated financial statements;
- its debt or equity instruments are not traded in a domestic or foreign public market (i.e. stock exchange);
- it did not file, nor is it in the process of filing, its financial statements with a securities commission or other regulatory organisation for the purpose of issuing any class of instruments in a public market; and
- its ultimate or any intermediate parent of the parent produces consolidated financial statements available for public use that comply with IFRSs.

Where consolidated financial statements are prepared, the consolidation procedures involve:

- combining like items of assets, liabilities, equity, income, expenses and cash flows of the parent with those of its subsidiaries from the date it gains control until the date when the reporting entity ceases to control the subsidiary;
- offsetting (i.e. eliminating) the carrying amount of the parent's investment in each subsidiary and the parent's portion of equity of each subsidiary (Chapter 26 of *Connolly* explains how to account for any related goodwill in accordance with IFRS 3 *Business Combinations*); and
- eliminating in full intra-group assets and liabilities, equity, income, expenses and cash flows relating to transactions between entities of the group, together with any profits or losses resulting from intragroup transactions that are recognised in assets, such as inventory and non-current.

Learning Objectives

By the end of Section Four you should understand:

- the principles and practices which underlie the preparation of a basic consolidated statement of financial position of a parent and one subsidiary;
- how to calculate goodwill and demonstrate how it is treated in a consolidated statement of financial position;
- the concept of non-controlling interests and how their share of the net assets of a subsidiary is calculated and disclosed;
- how to prepare and present a consolidated statement of financial position of a group consisting of a parent and one subsidiary, which would include the calculation of goodwill, non-controlling interests and unrealised profits in inventory.

Required Reading

Before attempting this section, you must read *Connolly*, Chapter 26: Business Combinations and Consolidated Financial Statements and Chapter 27: Consolidated Statement of Financial Position.

MEETINGS WITH YOUR PARTNER AND THE TEAM

You have completed the secondment at MCL and have returned to Shield Kenwick to continue your training. Your partner, Mr Ryan, has requested that you familiarise yourself with the terminology and the basic principles of preparing consolidated financial statements as he intends to include you in his team, which has a number of group clients. To this end, he has requested you to meet with the team once a week for two weeks. At each session you will report on three aspects relevant to the preparation and presentation of consolidated financial statements.

Task 20

Issues for First Meeting – 4 September 2013

Prepare a response to each of the following issues raised by your partner for the first meeting:

1. Why should we bother preparing consolidated financial statements? Do not a parent and a subsidiary prepare their individual financial statements?
2. What is the main criterion to be used to determine whether a parent has acquired a subsidiary?

3. You have been trained in presenting financial statements of an individual company in accordance with IAS 1 *Presentation of Financial Statements*. Do you now need to be familiar with a new layout?

Issues for Second Meeting – 11 September 2013

Prepare a response to each of the following issues raised by your partner for the second meeting:

1. You know all about goodwill since your involvement with the Poulenc Partnership. Is the goodwill you encountered then the same as that which arises in consolidated financial statements?
2. Now that you have garnered some very relevant information about groups and consolidated financial statements, your partner asks you: is there a difference between a company buying the net assets of another company and buying its shares?
3. What is understood by the term 'non-controlling interests'? How do non-controlling interests affect the consolidated statement of financial position?

Ethical Dilemma

You are engaged in the audit of a subsidiary and you make the following statement to another member of your firm who is your senior.

> "The subsidiary which I am auditing at the moment as part of a team looks pretty sick. The statement of financial position is pretty awful. The subsidiary has received very significant loans from its parent over the last two years and further amounts were given since the reporting date. I am worried about the going concern aspect."

Your senior replies to the effect that the rest of the group is very healthy and we the auditors will receive a written statement from the chairman that the parent and the other group companies will continue to provide financial support to the troubled subsidiary for commercial and strategic reasons. Can the firm rely on the word and subsequent written statement of the chairman?

POT LIMITED GROUP
PREPARATION OF CONSOLIDATED FINANCIAL STATEMENTS
For the Year Ended 30 September 2013

The following example involves the preparation and presentation of a consolidated statement of financial position for a group consisting of a parent Pot Ltd (Pot) and a subsidiary Stew Ltd (Stew) and requiring an adjustment to account for unrealised profit.

Instructions/Guidance

1. Begin with the individual financial statements of Pot and Stew (Section A).
2. Prepare the journal entry to treat the unrealised inventory profit (Section B).
3. Complete the statement of financial position workings and consolidation entries using the schedules prepared for either:
   - the T account method (Section C); or
   - the columnar method (Section D).
   (Your choice of method should be influenced by your lectures to date.)
4. Enter the final figures from your working schedules into the draft statement of financial position lead schedule (Section E).

CONTENTS

Section

A. Individual Statements of Financial Position of a parent (Pot Ltd) and a subsidiary (Stew Ltd)
B. Journal Entry
C. Workings for Statement of Financial Position using the T Account method
D. Workings for Statement of Financial Position using the columnar method
E. Consolidated Statement of Financial Position Lead Schedule

SECTION A: INDIVIDUAL STATEMENTS OF FINANCIAL POSITION

Statements of Financial Position of a Parent (Pot Ltd) and its Subsidiary Stew Ltd
as at 30 September 2013

	Pot €/£000	Stew €/£000
Assets		
Non-current assets		
Property, plant and equipment	5,600	2,160
Investment in Stew	1,260	0
Non-current assets		
Inventory	290	220
Trade receivables	330	250
Bank and cash	100	60
Total Assets	**7,580**	**2,690**
Equity and Liabilities		
Equity		
Ordinary share capital	4,000	1,000
Revaluation reserve	0	200
Retained earnings	3,010	1,050
Total equity	7,010	2,250
Non-current liabilities		
Trade payables	570	440
Total Equity and Liabilities	**7,580**	**2,690**

Relevant information:
1. Pot acquired 800,000 ordinary shares in Stew on 1 December 2010 when the retained earnings of Stew amounted to €/£550,000.
2. During September 2013 Stew sold goods to Pot at invoice value €/£150,000 on which the selling company earned a margin of 20%. One half of these goods was in the inventory of Pot at the reporting date.
3. The revaluation reserve arose in the year under review following a professional valuation of the property, plant and equipment of Stew Ltd.

SECTION B: JOURNAL ENTRY

Journal Entry (common to both T account and columnar methods)

		€/£000	€/£000
Journal 1	Debit		
	Credit		
	With the unrealised inventory profit		

SECTION C: WORKINGS – STATEMENT OF FINANCIAL POSITION – T ACCOUNT METHOD

Workings (T Account method)

Property, Plant and Equipment

Pot
Stew

Investment in Stew

Pot

Inventory

Pot
Stew

Trade Receivables

Pot
Stew

Bank and Cash

Pot
Stew

Trade Payables

| | Pot |
| | Stew |

Ordinary Shares

| | Pot |
| | Stew |

Revaluation Reserve

| | Stew |

Retained Earnings

| | Pot |
| | Stew |

Cost of Control

| | |

Non-controlling Interests (NCI)

| | |

SECTION D: WORKINGS – STATEMENT OF FINANCIAL POSITION – COLUMNAR METHOD

Workings (Columnar Method)

	Pot	Stew	Adjustments	Consol. SoFP
	€/£000	€/£000	€/£000	€/£000
Property, plant and equipment				
Investment in Stew				
Goodwill (*W1*)				
Inventory				
Trade receivables				
Bank and cash				
Total Assets				
Ordinary shares				
Revaluation reserve (*W2*)				
Retained earnings (*W3*)				
Non-controlling interests (*W4*)				
Trade payables				
Total Equity and Liabilities				

	€/£000	€/£000
(*W1*) Goodwill		
Cost of investment		
Stew at acquisition date		
Ordinary shares		
Retained earnings		
Group's share		
Consol. SoFP		
(*W2*) Revaluation reserve		
Stew		
Less non-controlling interests		
Consol. SoFP		
(*W3*) Retained earnings		
Pot at reporting date		
Stew		
At reporting date		
At acquisition date		
Post-acquisition		
Group's share		
Consol. SoFP		

(W4) Non-controlling interests
Stew at reporting date
Ordinary shares
Revaluation reserve
Retained earnings

SECTION E: CONSOLIDATED STATEMENT OF FINANCIAL POSITION LEAD SCHEDULE

Pot Limited
Consolidated Statement of Financial Position
as at 30 September 2013

Assets €/£000

Non-current assets
Property, plant and equipment
Goodwill

Current assets
Inventory
Trade receivables
Bank and cash

Total Assets

Equity and Liabilities

Equity
Ordinary share capital
Revaluation reserve
Retained earnings
Total shareholders' equity
Non-controlling interests
Total equity
Current liabilities
Trade payables
Total Equity and Liabilities

SUGGESTED SOLUTIONS

TASKS AND ETHICAL DILEMMAS

Suggested Solutions to Section One

SOLE TRADER:
JANE DOUGH – THE DOUGH HOUSE

Meeting 1 – 1 January 2012 – Response

Solution Task 1

1. Fundamental principles which underlie accounting A set of accounting records provides information for the day-to-day running of a business and for the periodic preparation of financial statements which show the profit or loss the business has made (income statement) and the position of the business at the end of the period (statement of financial position). Broadly speaking, the systematic recording and classifying of business transactions is called 'book-keeping' and this is governed by the application of well worn and generally accepted principles. The procedures adopted in book-keeping and the interpretation of the results obtained is called accounting. Accounting is thus a broader term than book-keeping and encompasses the term book-keeping since accounting determines the principles to be used, the records to be kept and the procedures to be followed. Broad accounting principles include:

(a) The Business Entity Principle This is one of the rules of book-keeping and there never is, nor can there be, any departure from it. This rule is that the business must be thought of as something completely separate and distinct from those who own it. You must always think in terms of what the business does and how it is affected by the things it does. Whatever the form of the business organisation may be – sole trader, partnership or limited company – for book-keeping purposes that organisation is a separate entity. So, with respect to The Dough House, we do not take into account your other activities (e.g. personal possessions and transactions).

(b) The Double Entry Concept (The Dual Aspect Concept) If a business is separate and distinct from its owners, it follows that a new business has nothing until it enters into obligations with its owners or with third parties. The very first obligation will usually be borrowing from the owner. The things owned by the business are called 'assets' and the amount owing to the proprietor is called 'capital'. In simple terms, in order to record an asset we must also acknowledge and record an amount owing in respect of that asset.

Thus, for everything owned there is a corresponding amount owing, i.e. there are two 'sides'. Each transaction that the business undertakes will require these two 'sides' and, therefore, two book-keeping entries – one to record the asset (the thing owned (debit)) and one to record the liability (the amount owing (credit)). For every debit there will be a corresponding credit.

2. Opening financial position of The Dough House

$$\text{Assets} = \text{Capital} + \text{Liabilities}$$

The assets of The Dough House are financed by Jane and a third party (the Building Society).

	€/£			€/£
Property	50,000		Capital	15,000
+			+	
Cash at bank	9,500	=	Building Society	45,000
+				
Cash-in-hand	500			
	60,000			60,000

Meeting 2 – End of Week 1, 2012 – Response

Tutorial Note As the goods for resale which cost €/£1,000 were bought on credit, the business owned another asset (the goods) but had another liability (the money owed to the supplier). The supplier to whom the business owes money is called a creditor, and the amount owed is shown as a 'payable' in the statement of financial position. This is classified as a 'current liability' as it is expected to be paid in this accounting period (i.e. within one year), in contrast to the mortgage on the premises which is classified as a non-current liability as it is repayable after more than one year *(ignore current year repayments at present)*.

At the end of the first week, the goods that remained unsold should be recorded as inventory (at the lower of cost and net realisable value), assuming that they are not perishable and could be resold at a later date. These goods are classified as a 'current asset' as they were purchased with the intention of turning them into cash in the ordinary course of business within one year. This is in contrast to the premises and fixtures and fittings which should be classified as 'non-current assets' as they were acquired for use within the business on a permanent basis.

As goods costing €/£900 were sold for €/£1,350, the business made a profit of €/£450. However, the €/£200 taken from the till to celebrate does not belong to Jane, it belongs to the business. Drawings is the term used for money (and goods) taken from a business by a proprietor (Jane) for their own personal use.

Assets = Proprietor's Interest (Capital + Profit − Drawings) + Liabilities

	€/£		€/£
Property	50,000	Capital	15,000
+		+	
Fixtures and fittings	2,500	Profit	450
+		−	
Inventory	100	Drawings	(200)
+		+	
Cash at bank	8,150	Payable	1,000
+		+	
Cash-in-hand	500	Building Society	45,000
	61,250		61,250

The accounting equation can also be expressed as:

Assets − Liabilities = Proprietor's Interest
or
Net Assets = Proprietor's Interest

The accounting equation forms the basis of one of the main financial statements of a business, i.e. the statement of financial position. The statement of financial position is a statement of the assets and liabilities of a business at a particular point in time.

Solution Task 2

The Dough House
STATEMENT OF FINANCIAL POSITION
as at End of Week One, 2012

	€/£	€/£
ASSETS		
Non-current Assets		
Property		50,000
Fixtures and fittings		2,500
		52,500
Current Assets		
Inventory	100	
Cash at bank	8,150	
Cash-in-hand	500	8,750
		61,250

EQUITY AND LIABILITIES
Capital	15,000
Profit for the period	450
	15,450
Less drawings	(200)
Proprietor's interests	15,250
Non-current Liabilities	
Mortgage	45,000
Current Liabilities	1,000
Trade payables	61,250

Meeting 3 – End of Week 3, 2012 – Response

Solution Task 3

At the end of week 1, the business's net assets (assets – liabilities) were €/£15,250. At the end of week 3, net assets were:

	€/£
Premises	50,000
Fixtures and fittings	2,500
Inventory	80
Cash at bank	8,000
Cash-in-hand	400
Mortgage	(45,000)
Trade payables	(850)
	15,130

During weeks 2 and 3, no capital was introduced and €/£520 (including goods for own use) was withdrawn from the business. Therefore, the profit made during weeks 2 and 3 amounted to:

Net Assets at end of period	–	Net Assets at beginning of period = decrease in Net Assets
€/£15,130	–	€/£15,250 = (€/£120)
Decrease in Net Assets	=	Capital Introduced + Profit – Drawings
(€/£120)	=	€/£0 + Profit – €/£520

Therefore the profit for weeks 2 and 3 = €/£400.

Meeting 4 – End of Month 2, 2012 – Response

Solution Task 4

Purchases Day Book

Date	Supplier Name	A/C No.	GIN No.	Net €/£	Vat €/£	Total €/£
1	Country Foods	201	1000	1,000	–	1,000
3	Fine Fare	202	1001	1,500	–	1,500
5	Country Foods	201	1002	1,200	–	1,200
5	Fine Fare	202	1003	1,400	–	1,400
11	Country Foods	201	1004	3,300	–	3,300
Total for period				8,400		8,400
				DR Purchases A/C		CR Payables A/C

Sales Day Book

Date	Customer Name	A/C No.	Invoice No.	Net €/£	Vat €/£	Total €/£
6	Cartwright	101	2001	2,200	–	2,200
12	Corpus	102	2002	2,500	–	2,500
Total for period				4,700		4,700
				CR Sales A/C		DR Receivables A/C

Cash Book

Debit Side:

Date	Narrative	Total €/£	Receivables Ledger €/£	Cash Sales €/£	Other Income €/£
2	Cash sales	1,350		1,350	
4	Cash sales	2,000		2,000	
7	Cash sales	1,400		1,400	
10	Cartwright	2,200	2,200		
13	Cash sales	2,300		2,300	
16	Cash sales	600		600	
Total for period		9,850	2,200	7,650	–
		DR Cash	CR Receivables Control A/C	CR Sales A/C	

Cash Book

Credit Side:

Date	Narrative	Total €/£	Payables Ledger €/£	Cash Purchase €/£	Other Income €/£
8	Country Foods (1000)	1,000	1,000		
9	Fine Fare (1001)	1,500	1,500		
14	Country Foods (1002)	1,200	1,200		
14	Fine Fare (1003)	1,400	1,400		
15	Goods (Chq. No. 33)	350		350	
–	Other expenses	10,400			10,400
Total for period		15,850	5,100	350	10,400
		CR Cash	DR Payables Control A/C	DR Purchases A/C	DR Other Expenses

Writing up the memorandum entries:

Country Foods Account (in payables ledger)

	€/£		€/£
8 Cash Book	1,000	1 PDB	1,000
14 Cash Book	1,200	5 PDB	1,200
		11 PDB	3,300
Bal. c/d	3,300		
	5,500		5,500
		Bal. b/d	3,300

Fine Fare Account (in payables ledger)

	€/£		€/£
9 Cash Book	1,500	3 PDB	1,500
14 Cash Book	1,400	5 PDB	1,400
Bal. c/d	–		
	2,900		2,900
		Bal. b/d	–

Cartwright Account (in receivables ledger)

	€/£		€/£
6 SDB	2,200	10 Cash Book	2,200
	2,200		2,200

Corpus Account (in receivables ledger)

	€/£		€/£
12 SDB	2,500	Bal. c/d	2,500
	2,500		2,500
Bal. b/d	2,500		

Writing up the ledger accounts (the double entry for the totals):

Receivables Control Account

	€/£		€/£
SDB	4,700	Cash Book	2,200
		Bal. c/d	2,500
	4,700		4,700
Bal. b/d	2,500		

Payables Control Account

	€/£		€/£
Cash Book	5,100	PDB	8,400
Bal. c/d	3,300		
	8,400		8,400
		Bal. b/d	3,300

Purchases Account

	€/£		€/£
PDB	8,400		
Cash Book	350	Bal. c/d	8,750
	8,750		8,750
Bal. b/d	8,750		

Sales Account

	€/£		€/£
Bal. c/d	12,350	SDB	4,700
	12,350	Cash Book	7,650
			12,350
		Bal. b/d	12,350

Cash Control Account

	€/£		€/£
O/bal	15,000	Cash Paid	15,850
Cash Rec'd	9,850	Bal. c/d	9,000
	24,850		24,850
Bal. b/d	9,000		

Tutorial Note The accounts making up the Payables Ledger are:

	Balance €/£
Country Foods	3,300
Fine Fare	–
Total per Receivables Ledger	3,300

This is equal to the balance on the Payables Control A/C.

The accounts making up the Receivables Ledger are:

	Balance €/£
Cartwright	–
Corpus	2,500
Total per Receivables Ledger	2,500

Only credit sales and credit purchases are recorded in the Sales Day Book and the Purchases Day Book. Cash sales and cash purchases are recorded in the cash book and at the end of the period (Month 2) have been posted to the sales account and purchases account as part of the double entry procedure.

The purchases account and sales account are not closed off at the end of the period (Month 2) since it is not the end of The Dough House's accounting period. The balances on these accounts are carried forward to the next period (Month 3). When further purchases and sales are made during this accounting period these will accumulate to give a total purchases and total sales figure to be transferred at the end of the accounting period to the income statement.

Ethical Dilemma – Response

Solution Task 5

(Leaving aside that you are a trainee accountant and, in reality, should simply refer the matter to your manager/partner, the principles involved are important.) The issue is one of confidentiality. While you should always be polite and courteous to the police, you also have a duty to your client. You should therefore ascertain under what authority they are requesting the information. If a search warrant is produced or they are acting under other statutory or court authority you must comply. If you are in any doubt, you should seek your own independent legal advice.

If you are unfamiliar with the legal documentation and/or you are unable to obtain your client's authority you may wish to obtain your own legal advice as to the legal effect of such documentation and your own position before taking any further action.

In all other situations, you should explain to the police that under the rules of your professional body you are not in a position to discuss your client's affairs without their authority or appropriate statutory or court authority.

The only times you can divulge information about a client without their authority is:

- when those requesting the information have statutory authority;
- it is in the public interest; and
- to protect your own interests in certain circumstances.

In addition to the police, examples of other appropriately empowered authorities could include taxation authorities, fire authorities, health and safety and those empowered under local jurisdictions.

Meeting 5 – End of Month 4, 2012 – Response

Solution Task 6

The action required to correct the errors are:

				€/£	€/£
(a)	DR		Corpus Limited's individual sales ledger a/c	240	
		CR	Corpus Limited's individual payables ledger a/c		240

Being the memorandum entries required to correct the misposting (adjust the list of balances for this).

(b)	DR		Sales Ledger Control a/c	310	
		CR	Sales Account		310

Being the double entry required to record the omitted invoice. (Also, correct Cartwright Limited's individual Sales Ledger a/c and adjust the list of balances for this.)

(c)	DR		Payables Control a/c	100	
		CR	Sales Ledger Control a/c		100

Being the double entry required to reflect the contra entry to Mission Limited's accounts.

(d) Add in the debit balance of €/£400 omitted from the list of balances.

(e) Deduct €/£540 from the list of balances and make a credit entry to this amount on the relevant customer's individual account.

(f) Credit Morricone Limited's individual ledger account with the €/£500 cash received from them and take this amount away from the list of balances.

(g)	DR		Sales Account	220	
		CR	Sales Ledger Control Account		220

Being the double entry required to reverse the €/£220 too much previously posted due to an overcast SDB.

The adjusted Sales Ledger Control Account is:

Sales Ledger Control Account

	€/£		€/£
Bal. b/d	9,345		
Invoice omitted (b)	310	Contra to	
		Payables Ledger (c)	100
		Overcast SDB (g)	220
		Bal. c/d	9,335
	9,655		9,655
Bal. b/d	9,335		

The corrected total list of balances:

	€/£
Original total list of balances	9,425
Sales to Corpus Limited (a)	240
Invoice omitted (b)	310
Omitted debit balance (d)	400
Transposition error (e)	(540)
Cash not recorded (f)	(500)
Corrected total list of balances	9,335

Solution Task 7

Purchase Ledger Control Account

	€/£		€/£
		Bal. b/d	8,445
Contra to		Undercast PDB (a)	650
Receivables ledger (b)	400	Country Foods (c)	135
Balance c/d	8,830		
	9,230		9,230
		Balance b/d	9,230

	€/£
Original total list of balances	8,870
Invoice not recorded (c)	850
Cash paid not recorded (d)	(700)
Credit balance omitted (e)	450
Sales to Corpus Limited (f)	(240)
Corrected total list of balances	9,230

Solution Task 8

There are two separate parts of a bank reconciliation to perform. First, correcting the cash book for errors made and, secondly, adjusting the bank statement balances for timing differences and bank errors (if applicable).

Cash Book

	€/£		€/£
Bal. b/d	8,100	Direct debit (c)	250
Credit transfer (d)	650	Bal. c/d	8,500
	8,750		8,750
Bal. b/d	8,500		

	€/£
Balance per bank statement	5,650
Add: Deposits not cleared	6,500
Less: Unpresented cheques	(3,650)
Balance per cash book	8,500

It is important to realise that when The Dough House business deposits money with the bank (a receipt) it will debit its cash book but the bank will show that receipt as a credit. This is quite logical if you consider that the business has more money (an increase in an asset) and must therefore make a debit entry while from the bank's point of view they debit their cash book and credit the account of the business. The bank 'owes' The Dough House the money and therefore the bank is a creditor from their perspective. Similarly, when a business has an account which is overdrawn it will owe money to the bank so the cash book will show a credit balance but the bank will have a debtor. When you are told that a bank account is 'in credit' it means there is money in the account since you are being told the position from the bank's point of view.

Ethical Dilemma – Response

Solution Task 9

This is an issue of potential conflict of interest. Would a reasonable and informed third party having knowledge of all the relevant information reasonably conclude that your independence was compromised? Have you actually been influenced in your professional judgement as a result of your client's offer?

It is necessary to establish the facts of the case. For example, is the client offering a discount greater than that currently being offered? Is it greater than the discount to which her members of staff are entitled on a regular basis? Indeed, is it a 'good price' merely by reference to other retailers and is it in fact her 'normal' list price?

Even if the offer made by the client is specific to you, her accountant, the quantum of the benefit is likely to be relevant. If the effective discount is a flat rate 10%, whatever the list price of the jewellery bought, then it is unlikely that an informed third party would regard that your independence was compromised. In addition to the ethical guidance of Chartered Accountants Ireland, you should also refer to your employer's internal policies and contractual obligations. Moreover, common sense should dictate that it would be sensible to clarify your position with your employer.

Independence of mind is the state of mind that permits the provision of an opinion without being affected by influences that compromise professional judgement, allowing an individual to act with integrity and exercise objectivity and professional scepticism. Independence in appearance requires you to avoid facts and circumstances that are so significant that a reasonable and informed third party, having knowledge of all relevant information, including safeguards applied, would reasonably conclude that integrity, objectivity, and professional scepticism had been compromised. Thus, it can be seen that there are circumstances when your client's offer may not compromise your integrity, especially as you are a trainee accountant.

However, there are others where your integrity could be called into doubt: the more senior your position in the firm, the greater the risk of this occurring. It may however be possible to ensure that safeguards are put in place to protect your independence. These might include an independent review of any work undertaken, the work to be undertaken by qualified staff within your firm and not directly under your influence, rotation of the partner in charge and the senior staff. The appropriate safeguards will depend on: your position within the firm; the size and circumstances of the practice and the client; and the perceived threat to your independence.

Variation on the Issue   If you were working for a department store and your supplier, the owner of the jewellery store, made you the same offer, there might still be a conflict of interest. As an employee of the department store, you could be in a situation to influence and repay the favour, perhaps by ensuring that the department store gave her a favourable contract. The significance of such a threat would depend on the nature and value of the offer and the intent behind it. In addition to the Institute's ethical guidance, you should also refer to your employer's internal policies and contractual obligations.

Meeting 6 – End of Month 6, 2012 – Response

Solution Task 10

Capital

	€/£		€/£
		Bal. b/d	15,000
Bal. c/d	15,000		
	15,000		15,000
		Bal. b/d	15,000

Drawings

	€/£		€/£
O/B	5,100		
30/6 Bank	1,000	Bal. c/d	6,100
	6,100		6,100
Bal. b/d	6,100		

Building Society Mortgage

	€/£		€/£
30/6 Bank	250	Bal. b/d	43,750
Bal. c/d	43,875	30/6 Interest	375
	44,125		44,125
		Bal. b/d	43,875

Repayments:	€/£
12 × 20 years × €/£250	60,000
Initial advance	45,000
Interest	15,000
/ 20 years	750 p.a.
/ 12	62.50 pm SL

			€/£	€/£
DR		IS – interest (6 months)	375	
	CR	Mortgage		375

		€/£
Mortgage balance		43,875
12 × (€/£250 – €/£62.50)	< 1 year	(2,250)
	> 1 year	41,625

Purchases

		€/£			€/£
	Bal. b/d	24,600			
1/6	C. Foods	400	11/6	Filler	200
1/6	Filler	1,200			
1/6	F. Fare	1,350		Bal. c/d	27,350
		27,550			27,550
	Bal. b/d	27,350			

Fine Fare Limited

		€/£			€/£
				Bal. b/d	910
	Bal. c/d	2,260	1/6	Purchases	1,350
		2,260			2,260
				Bal. b/d	2,260

Fixtures and Fittings

		€/£			€/£
	Bal. b/d	2,500			
2/6	Bank	500		Bal. c/d	3,000
		3,000			3,000
	Bal. b/d	3,000			

Insurance

		€/£			€/£
	Bal. b/d	300	20/6	Bank	100
5/6	Bank	160		Bal. c/d	360
		460			460
	Bal. b/d	360			

Morricone Limited

		€/£			€/£
7/6	Sales	500	14/6	Credit note	40
			17/6	Bank	460
		500			500

Bank

		€/£			€/£
	Bal. b/d	8,000	2/6	Fittings	500
7/6	Cash sales	1,580	5/6	Insurance	160
14/6	Cash sales	1,610	7/6	Wages	100
21/6	Cash sales	1,575	10/6	Heat and light	50
28/6	Cash sales	1,645	9/6	Postage and telephone	75
17/6	Morricone	460	12/6	Ball	100
20/6	Insurance	100	21/6	Wages	100
25/6	Banks	220	28/6	Filler	1,200
25/6	Cartwright	100	28/6	Postage and telephone	75
			28/6	Wages	100
			30/6	Van	6,000
			30/6	Mortgage	250
			30/6	Drawings	1,000

				Bal. c/d	5,580
		15,290			15,290
	Bal. b/d	5,580			

Corpus Limited

		€/£			€/£
	Bal. b/d	380			
7/6	Sales	300		Bal. c/d	680
		680			680
	Bal. b/d	680			

Ball Limited

		€/£			€/£
12/6	Bank	100	8/6	Stationery	100
		100			100

Heat and Light

		€/£			€/£
	Bal. b/d	250			
10/6	Bank	50		Bal. c/d	300
		300			300
	Bal. b/d	300			

Mission Limited

		€/£			€/£
	Bal. b/d	500			
13/6	Sales	270		Bal. c/d	770
		770			770
	Bal. b/d	770			

Cash

		€/£			€/£
	Bal. b/d	500	15/6	Wages	120
			21/6	General expenses	50
				Bal. c/d	330
		500			500
	Bal. b/d	330			

Country Foods

		€/£			€/£
				Bal. b/d	850
	Bal. c/d	1,250	1/6	Purchases	400
		1,250			1,250
				Bal. b/d	1,250

Filler Limited

		€/£			€/£
				Bal. b/d	200
11/6	Returns	200	1/6	Purchases	1,200
28/6	Bank	1,200		Bal. c/d	-
		1,400			1,400

Premises

		€/£			€/£
	Bal. b/d	50,000		Bal. c/d	50,000
		50,000			50,000
	Bal. b/d	50,000			

Delivery Van

		€/£			€/£
30/6	Bank	6,000		Bal. c/d	6,000
		6,000			6,000
	Bal. b/d	6,000			

Cartwright Limited

		€/£			€/£
	Bal. b/d	420			
7/6	Sales	400	25/6	Bank	100
13/6	Sales	150		Bal. c/d	870
		970			970
	Bal. b/d	870			

Sales

		€/£			€/£
				Bal. b/d	34,750
14/6	Morricone	40	7/6	Cash sales	1,580
			7/6	Morricone	500
			7/6	Cartwright	400
			7/6	Corpus	300
			13/6	Banks	220
			13/6	Cartwright	150
			13/6	Mission	270
			14/6	Cash sales	1,610
			21/6	Cash sales	1,575
			28/6	Cash sales	1,645
	Bal. c/d	42,960			
		43,000			43,000
				Bal. b/d	42,960

Stationery and Advertising

		€/£		€/£
	Bal. b/d	660		
8/6	Ball Ltd	100	Bal. c/d	760
		760		760
	Bal. b/d	760		

Postage and Telephone

		€/£		€/£
	Bal. b/d	150		
13/6	Bank	75		
28/6	Bank	75	Bal. c/d	300
		300		300
	Bal. b/d	300		

Banks Limited

		€/£			€/£
9/6	Sales	220	25/6	Bank	220
		220			220

Wages

		€/£		€/£
	Bal. b/d	2,000		
7/6	Bank	100		
15/6	Cash	120		
21/6	Bank	100		
28/6	Bank	100	Bal. c/d	2,420
		2,420		2,420
	Bal. b/d	2,420		

General Expenses

		€/£		€/£
	Bal. b/d	100		
21/6	Cash	50	Bal. c/d	150
		150		150
	Bal. b/d	150		

The Dough House
Trial Balance
as at 30 June 2012

	DR €/£	CR €/£
Premises – at cost	50,000	
Delivery van – at cost	6,000	
Fixtures and fittings – at cost	3,000	
Mortgage (€/£45,000 − (6 × €/£250) + €/£375)		43,875
Drawings	6,100	
Capital		15,000
Bank	5,580	
Cash	330	
Purchases	27,350	
Trade payable – Country Foods Limited		1,250
Trade payable – Filler Limited		–
Trade payable – Fine Fare Limited		2,260
Insurance (€/£60 per month)	360	
Sales		42,960
Trade receivable – Cartwright Limited	870	
Trade receivable – Corpus Limited	680	
Trade receivable – Mission Limited	770	
Stationery and advertising	760	
Postage and telephone	300	
Heat and light	300	
Staff wages	2,420	

Mortgage interest	375	
General expenses	150	
	105,345	105,345

The Dough House
Income Statement
for the Six-month Period Ended 30 June 2012

	€/£	€/£
Sales		42,960
Cost of Sales:		
Opening inventory	–	
Purchases	27,350	
Closing inventory	(200)	(27,150)
Gross profit		15,810
Expenses:		
Insurance	360	
Stationery and advertising	760	
Postage and telephone	300	
Heat and light	300	
Staff wages	2,420	
Mortgage interest	375	
General expenses	150	(4,665)
Net profit		11,145

The Dough House
Statement of Financial Position
as at 30 June 2012

	€/£	€/£
ASSETS		
Non-current Assets		
Premises		50,000
Delivery van		6,000
Fixtures and fittings		3,000
		59,000
Current Assets		
Inventory	200	
Trade receivables – Cartwright Limited	870	
Trade receivables – Corpus Limited	680	
Trade receivables – Mission Limited	770	
Bank	5,580	
Cash	330	8,430
		67,430

OWNER'S INTEREST AND LIABILITIES

Owner's Interest

Capital		15,000
Profit		11,145
Drawings		(6,100)
		20,045

Non-current Liabilities

Mortgage		41,625

Current Liabilities

Trade payables – Country Foods Limited	1,250	
Trade payables – Filler Limited	–	
Trade payables – Fine Fare Limited	2,260	
Mortgage	2,250	5,760
		67,430

Meeting 7 – Early January 2013 – Response

Solution Task 11

The Dough House
INCOME STATEMENT
for the Year Ended 31 December 2012

	€/£	€/£
Sales		89,600
Cost of Sales:		
Opening inventory	–	
Purchases	56,400	
Closing inventory	(250)	(56,150)
Gross profit		33,450
Expenses:		
Depreciation – premises (2% × €/£50,000)	1,000	
Depreciation – delivery van (25% × €/£6,000)	1,500	
Depreciation – fixtures and fittings (20% × €/£4,000)	800	
Allowance for irrecoverable debts (10% × €/£650)	65	
Insurance (€/£780 – €/£60 prepayment)	720	
Stationery and advertising	900	
Postage and telephone	400	
Heat and light (€/£950 + €/£80 accrual)	1,030	
Staff wages	5,775	
Mortgage interest (12 × €/£62.50)	750	
General expenses (€/£600 – €/£50 drawings)	550	(13,490)
Net profit		19,960

The Dough House
Statement of Financial Position
as at 31 December 2012

	€/£	€/£
ASSETS		
Non-current Assets		
Premises (€/£50,000 − €/£1,000 depreciation)		49,000
Delivery van (€/£6,000 − €/£1,500 depreciation)		4,500
Fixtures and fittings (€/£4,000 − €/£800)		3,200
		56,700
Current Assets		
Inventory	250	
Trade receivables – Cartwright Limited	550	
Trade receivables – Corpus Limited	500	
Trade receivables – Mission Limited	600	
Trade receivables – Other (€/£650 − €/£65)	585	
Prepayments – insurance	60	
Bank	6,100	
Cash	300	8,945
		65,645
OWNER'S INTEREST AND LIABILITIES		
Owner's Interest		
Capital		15,000
Profit		19,960
Drawings (€/£16,000 + €/£50)		(16,050)
		18,910
Non-current Liabilities		
Mortgage (18 years × 12 months × (€/£250 − €/£62.50))		40,500
Current Liabilities		
Trade payables – Country Foods Limited	1,200	
Trade payables – Filler Limited	905	
Trade payables – Fine Fare Limited	1,800	
Accruals – heat and light	80	
Mortgage (12 months × (€/£250 − €/£62.50)	2,250	6,235
		65,645

Suggested Solutions to Section Two

PARTNERSHIP: THE POULENC PARTNERSHIP

Meeting 1 – 31 January 2013 – Response

Solution Task 12

The Poulenc Partnership
Income Statement
for the Year Ended 31 December 2012

	€/£	€/£
Sales		650,000
Opening inventory	78,000	
Purchases	380,000	
Carriage inwards	4,000	
	462,000	
Less: Closing inventory	(71,000)	(391,000)
Gross profit		259,000
General expenses	36,000	
Carriage outwards	5,000	
Depreciation	6,000	(47,000)
Net profit		212,000

The Poulenc Partnership
STATEMENT OF FINANCIAL POSITION
as at 31 December 2012

	Cost €/£	Acc depn €/£	€/£
ASSETS			
Non-current Assets			
Premises	80,000	(14,000)	66,000
Fixtures and fittings	24,000	(10,000)	14,000
			80,000
Current Assets			
Inventory		71,000	
Trade receivables		168,000	
Cash		50,000	289,000
			369,000
OWNERSHIP INTEREST AND LIABILITIES			
Ownership Interest			
Partners' accounts	Capital accounts €/£	Current accounts €/£	€/£
Maire Louise Phillips	45,000	25,250	70,250
Joseph Phillips	40,000	14,450	54,450
Christopher Pringle	34,000	25,000	59,000
Caiti Pollen	50,000	31,750	81,750
Ellen Peterson	26,000	25,550	51,550
	195,000	122,000	317,000
Current Liabilities			
Trade payables			52,000
			369,000

Partners' Current Accounts

	MLP €/£	JP €/£	CPr €/£	CPo €/£	EP €/£		MLP €/£	JP €/£	CPr €/£	CPo €/£	EP €/£
2012						2012					
Drawings	35,000	25,000	22,000	30,000	18,000	O/b	10,000	8,000	7,000	11,000	4,000
Bal. c/d	25,250	14,450	25,000	31,750	25,550	IS	50,250	31,450	40,000	50,750	39,550
	60,250	39,450	47,000	61,750	43,550		60,250	39,450	47,000	61,750	43,550
						Bal. b/d	25,250	14,450	25,000	31,750	25,550

Workings

Having calculated the profit for the year, it has to be appropriated between the partners.

	MLP €/£	JP €/£	CPr €/£	CPo €/£	EP €/£
Interest on capital at 10%	4,500	4,000	3,400	5,000	2,600
Salaries	-	-	-	-	9,500
Balance of profit (€/£212,000 − €/£29,000)	45,750	27,450	36,600	45,750	27,450
	50,250	31,450	40,000	50,750	39,550

Ethical Dilemma – Response

Solution Task 13

This is a client identification matter. Your firm must carry out the same identification procedures it would with any new client. Your firm will need to identify the parent company to the extent that it knows who runs the company and verify that they are authorised to instruct your client.

If your firm is unable to do this itself then it will need to instruct an appropriately qualified firm, such as a member of Chartered Accountants Ireland in that country, or ask them to suggest a lawyer who can undertake the verification on its behalf. They will need to send your firm certified copies of all original documentation seen by them. The verification will include: the structure of the parent company, letters of incorporation filed with the government, lists of board members, and other publicly available material.

If your firm cannot verify the ownership, ultimate control or significant influence over the business and its assets, it is likely to result in your firm not accepting the appointment.

Your firm should also be aware of relevant guidance on money laundering.

Meeting 2 – 28 February 2013 – Response

Solution Task 14

Briefing Note

Measurement of Goodwill There can be no precise valuation of goodwill, which has to be essentially the result of an exercise of judgement of the worth of the business as a whole by the parties involved.

Accounting Treatment There are two main situations as regards goodwill:

1. The partners wish to include goodwill as an asset in their statement of financial position, which is the least likely situation in practice.

In this situation use can be made of the revaluation account:

Debit	Credit	With
Goodwill	Revaluation	Increase in the value of goodwill
Revaluation	Goodwill	Decrease in the value of goodwill

If goodwill has not previously been incorporated in the books, the entry is:

| Debit | Credit | With |
| Goodwill | Revaluation | The agreed value of goodwill |

Quite often, it is only goodwill that is required to be revalued. The book value of the assets may be fairly close to their market value and thus the time and expense involved in making valuations is too much compared to the benefits.

If only goodwill is being revalued, the revaluation account need not be used. The revaluation increase (or decrease) can be transferred from the goodwill account to the partner's capital accounts.

2. The partners do not wish to include goodwill as an asset in their balance sheet but the effect of goodwill needs to be reflected in their capital accounts.

In many cases, goodwill will not be shown on the statement of financial position after a partnership change despite the fact that a new partner, for example, has paid for a share. There are a number of reasons why partnerships do not wish to record goodwill in the statement of financial position:

(a) *Subjective Nature of Valuation* The value attached to goodwill on a partnership change is either a matter of negotiation between the partners or derived from a formula in the partnership agreement. It only represents a value attached to the asset at the time of the change. In changing business conditions in the future its value may be very different.

(b) *Taxation* For capital gains tax purposes it is generally disadvantageous to record partnership goodwill as an asset.

(c) *Amortisation (depreciation)* If goodwill is recorded as an asset should it not be depreciated like any other non-current asset? Some would say yes and some no. The argument is however avoided if goodwill is not shown in the first place.

This will not change the need to make entries – the old partners by allowing another person into partnership are sharing their business with him. They are thus selling some of the past goodwill to him and this fact needs to be recorded in the capital accounts.

Ethical Dilemma – Response

Solution Task 15

In all circumstances, the membership regulations of Chartered Accountants Ireland and the standards of the jurisdiction in which you practise take precedence over the requirements of any network your firm may be a member of. Your firm must therefore comply with all the relevant Auditing and Ethical Standards and membership rules of Chartered Accountants Ireland in full. The firm cannot rely on the fact that 'the client is well-known to the network'. If your firm agrees to do the work, it will need to undertake a full audit, as it would do if the client had been referred from any other source. Only then can your firm put its signature to the report.

Meeting 3 – 3 January 2014 – Response

Solution Task 16

The Poulenc Partnership
INCOME STATEMENT
for Year Ended 31 December 2013

	€/£	€/£
Sales		750,000
Cost of sales:		
Opening inventory	71,000	
Purchases	400,000	
	471,000	
Closing inventory (note 1)	(81,000)	
		(390,000)
Gross profit		360,000
Expenses:		
General expenses (per TB)	40,000	
Accruals (note 4)	3,215	
Allowance for irrecoverable debts (note 3)	3,535	
Depreciation (note 2)	14,000	
		(60,750)
		299,250
Capital grant release (note 5)		350
Net profit		299,600

The Poulenc Partnership
Statement of Financial Position
as at 31 December 2013

	€/£	€/£
ASSETS		
Non-current Assets (note 2)		
Premises		200,500
Fixtures and fittings		32,500
		233,000
Current Assets		
Inventory	81,000	
Trade receivables (note 3)	166,465	
Capital grant receivable	14,000	
Cash at bank and in hand	98,000	
		359,465
		592,465
OWNERSHIP INTEREST AND LIABILITIES		
Ownership Interest		
Partners' accounts		449,855
Non-current Liabilities		
Partner's loan account		65,745
Deferred credit (note 5)		13,650
Current Liabilities		
Trade payables	60,000	
Accruals (note 4)	3,215	
		63,215
		592,465

Partners' Accounts

	MLP €/£	JP €/£	CPr €/£	CPo €/£	EP €/£	JD €/£
O/balance	45,000	40,000	34,000	50,000	26,000	–
Capital introduced	–	–	–	–	–	50,000
Current a/c	57,213	16,745	57,370	70,213	58,377	10,682
G'will (old) (note 7)	15,000	9,000	12,000	15,000	9,000	–
G'will (new) (note 7)	(15,000)	–	(12,000)	(15,000)	(9,000)	(9,000)
Transfer to loan a/c	–	(65,745)	–	–	–	–
	102,213	–	91,370	120,213	84,377	51,682

Total 449,855

Partners' Current Accounts

	MLP €/£	JP €/£	CPr €/£	CPo €/£	EP €/£	JD €/£		MLP €/£	JP €/£	CPr €/£	CPo €/£	EP €/£	JD €/£
Drawings	40,000	20,000	25,000	34,000	20,000	12,000	O/bal	25,250	14,450	25,000	31,750	25,550	–
							Salary	–	–	–	–	4,750	–
							Interest	2,250	2,000	1,700	2,500	1,300	–
							Profit	33,825	20,295	27,060	33,825	20,295	–
							Salary	–	–	–	–	5,000	–
							Interest	2,250	–	1,700	2,500	1,300	2,500
C/bal	57,213	16,745	57,370	70,213	58,377	10,682	Profit	33,638	–	26,910	33,638	20,182	20,182
	97,213	36,745	82,370	104,213	78,377	22,682		97,213	36,745	82,370	104,213	78,377	22,682

Note 1: Inventory   €/£   €/£

	€/£	€/£
Per inventory take		90,000
15% at cost	(13,500)	
Net realisable value	8,500	
		(5,000)
Obsolete inventory		(4,000)
Revised closing inventory		81,000

Note 2: Depreciation

	Depreciation €/£	NBV €/£
Premises – cost at 1 January 2013		80,000
Premises – additions during 2013		140,000
		220,000
Depreciation – straight line over 40 years	(5,500)	(5,500)
Accumulated depreciation at 1 January 2013		(14,000)
Net book value of premises at 31 December 2013		200,500
Fixtures and fittings – cost at 1 January 2013		24,000
Fixtures and fittings – additions during 2013		27,000
		51,000
Depreciation – straight line over 6 years	(8,500)	(8,500)
Accumulated depreciation at 1 January 2013		(10,000)
Net book value of fixtures and fittings at 31 December 2013		32,500

Note 3: Trade receivables

	€/£	€/£
Trade receivables as per TB		170,000
Irrecoverable debt	(1,000)	(1,000)
		169,000
Allowance for irrecoverable debts @ 1.5%	(2,535)	(2,535)
Revised receivables at 31 December 2013		166,465

Note 4: Accruals

	€/£	€/£
Dr Income Statement – general expenses	3,215	
Cr Statement of Financial Position – accruals		3,215

	€/£	€/£
Note 5: Capital grant		
Grant receivable		14,000
Release to income statement over 40 years	350	(350)
Deferred credit for statement of financial position at 31 December 2013		13,650

	€/£	€/£
Note 6: Profit split		
Profit for year		299,600
First 6 months	149,800	
Less: Salary – Ellen €/£9,500 × 6/12	(4,750)	
Interest on capital @10% × 6/12:		
Maire Louise Phillips	(2,250)	
Joseph Phillips	(2,000)	
Christopher Pringle	(1,700)	
Caiti Pollen	(2,500)	
Ellen Peterson	(1,300)	
	135,300	
Allocated to partners: old ratio		
Maire Louise Phillips: 25%	33,825	
Joseph Phillips: 15%	20,295	
Christopher Pringle: 20%	27,060	
Caiti Pollen: 25%	33,825	
Ellen Peterson: 15%	20,295	
	135,300	
Second 6 months	149,800	
Less: Salary – Ellen €/£10,000 x 6/12	(5,000)	
Interest on capital @10% x 6/12:		
Maire Louise Phillips	(2,250)	
Christopher Pringle	(1,700)	
Caiti Pollen	(2,500)	
Ellen Peterson	(1,300)	
Jane Dough	(2,500)*	
	134,550	
Allocated to partners: new ratio		
Maire Louise Phillips: 25%	33,638	
Christopher Pringle: 20%	26,910	
Caiti Pollen: 25%	33,638	
Ellen Peterson: 15%	20,182	
Jane Dough: 15%	20,182	
	134,550	

* Interest on capital for Jane Dough could be calculated excluding goodwill, i.e. €/£41,000 × 10% × 6/12 = £2,050.

Note 7: Goodwill
Jane Dough's share of goodwill = €/£9,000 = 15%.
Therefore total partnership goodwill = €/£60,000.

	Old €/£	New €/£
Maire Louise Phillips – 25%	15,000	15,000
Joseph Phillips – 15%	9,000	–
Christopher Pringle – 20%	12,000	12,000
Caiti Pollen – 25%	15,000	15,000
Ellen Peterson – 15%	9,000	9,000
Jane Dough – 15%	–	9,000

Meeting 4 – 31 January 2014

Solution Task 17

			DR €/£	CR €/£
DR		Realisation account	592,465	
	CR	Assets taken over		592,465
		– being book value of assets taken over		
DR		Liabilities taken over	142,610	
	CR	Realisation account		142,610
		– being book value of liabilities taken over		
DR		Realisation account	50,000	
	CR	Maire Louise Phillips		12,500
		Christopher Pringle		10,000
		Caiti Pollen		12,500
		Ellen Peterson		7,500
		Jane Dough		7,500
		– being increase in valuation of premises and fixtures and fittings taken over		
DR		Poulenc Company Limited	499,855	
	CR	Realisation account		499,855
		– being agreed value of assets and liabilities taken over		
DR		Partners' current accounts	253,855	
	CR	Partners' capital accounts		253,855
		– being transfer of partners' current accounts to their capital accounts		

DR		Maire Louise Phillips	114,713
DR		Christopher Pringle	101,370
DR		Caiti Pollen	132,713
DR		Ellen Peterson	91,877
DR		Jane Dough	59,182
	CR	Poulenc Company Limited	499,855

– being allocation of ordinary share capital in Poulenc Company Limited to partners in proportion to the final balances on their capital accounts

Poulenc Company Limited
STATEMENT OF FINANCIAL POSITION
as at 1 January 2014

	€/£	€/£
ASSETS		
Non-current Assets		
Premises		250,000
Fixtures and fittings		33,000
		283,000
Current Assets		
Inventory	81,000	
Trade receivables	166,465	
Capital grant receivable	14,000	
Cash at bank and on hand	98,000	
		359,465
		642,465
CAPITAL AND LIABILITIES		
Capital		
€/£1 ordinary shares		499,855
Non-current Liabilities		
Loan account		65,745
Deferred credit		13,650
Current Liabilities		
Trade payables	60,000	
Accruals	3,215	
		63,215
		642,465

Ethical Dilemma – Response

Solution Task 18

As adviser to the partnership, and both the individual partners, your firm has a responsibility to provide balanced advice and avoid any conflict of interest. The key issues to be addressed are:

- What is the real issue?
- Are there threats to compliance with fundamental principles?
- Are the threats clearly significant?
- Are there safeguards that will eliminate the threats or reduce them to an acceptable level? and
- Can you face yourself in the mirror?

What is the real issue? The partners relying on the accounts to determine the amount due to the outgoing partner when there are assets which are not reflected at their current value in the statement of financial position is not in itself unfair to the outgoing partner. Your firm should take the following steps to establish whether or not there is any reason to be uneasy:

1. Look to the partnership agreement, if one exists, to determine the basis on which the partnership should be dissolved. This may also contain details of the basis on which the property was brought into the partnership accounts.
2. If there is no partnership agreement, it will be necessary to look to any partnership law for the jurisdiction in which the partnership falls to see if this sets out how the assets are to be distributed on the dissolution of the partnership.
3. In many jurisdictions, interests in land are held outside the partnership. It might therefore be necessary to look to the title deeds and any ancillary agreement relating thereto.
4. It should also be noted that individuals are free to enter into such arrangements as they see fit; after all, one partner could gift their share of the partnership to the other. You need to establish if the partners have arrived at this basis for dissolving the partnership because of specific circumstances. For example, the partners may have agreed when they first went into partnership that, although they held the property in joint names, the continuing partner would be entitled to any increase in value in the property because he/she had provided all the original capital.

Are there threats to compliance with fundamental principles? A threat to objectivity or confidentiality may be created when members perform services for clients whose interests are in conflict or the clients are in dispute with each other in relation to the matter (or transaction) in question. Therefore, if after considering all of the above, your firm believes that the partner who is leaving has not made an informed decision to accept the balance standing to his credit in the statement of financial position there may be a conflict of interests between the two partners with regard to the basis on which the partnership should be dissolved.

Where such a situation arises, all reasonable steps should be taken to ascertain whether any conflict of interest exists, or is likely to arise in the future, both in regard to new engagements and to the changing circumstances of existing clients, and including any implications arising from the possession of confidential information. There is, on the face of it, nothing improper in firms having two or more clients whose interests may be in conflict, provided that the work the firm undertakes is not in itself likely to be the subject of dispute between those clients.

Are the threats clearly significant? If, after following the previous steps, it is clear that there is a conflict of interest then this will be significant because the accounts that your firm has prepared are likely to form the basis of agreement between the partners. It is important to remember that perceived threats are as relevant as actual threats. The underlying test is whether a reasonable and informed third party, having knowledge of all relevant information, including the safeguards applied, would conclude that a firm's integrity, objectivity or professional scepticism had been compromised.

Are there safeguards that will eliminate the threats or reduce them to an acceptable level? If you are in a large practice, it might be possible to put safeguards in place by ensuring that different partners acted for the different parties. However, a sole practitioner for example, if it is established that there is a conflict of interest between the partners, would no longer be able to act for all three parties (the two partners and the business) since the accounts prepared by him are likely to become drawn into any dispute between the partners as to their rights on the dissolution. If a sole practitioner (or small practice) were to continue to act for both of the individual partners, it could be forced into a position where it had to choose between the interests of different clients. Ideally a meeting should be arranged at which both partners are present so that the position can be explained to them, one or both being advised to take independent professional advice on the dissolution of the partnership. If this is not possible, your firm should write to both partners setting out the position.

Can you face yourself in the mirror? Having followed these steps, it is likely that your unease will have been resolved and you can indeed 'face yourself in the mirror'. It may be, however, that there are circumstances which still leave you feeling uneasy. In that case, you may have no alternative but to cease to act for any of the parties.

Suggested Solutions to Section Three

LIMITED COMPANY: MY COMPANY LIMITED (MCL)

Solution Task 19

Coffee – 31 January 2012 – Response

Revenue is often discussed in terms of inflows of assets to an organisation that occur as a result of outflows of goods and services from that organisation. Consequently, the concept of revenue recognition has traditionally been associated with specific accounting procedures that are primarily directed towards determining the timing and measurement of revenue. Accordingly, the revenue recognition debate has taken place in the context of the historical cost double entry system, with accounting principles focusing on determining when transactions should be recognised in the financial statements, what amounts are involved in each transaction, how these amounts should be classified and how they should be allocated between accounting periods.

Historical cost accounting in its pure form avoids having to take a valuation approach to financial reporting by virtue of the fact that it is transaction based, i.e. it relies on transactions to determine recognition and measurement of assets, liabilities, revenues and expenses. Over an organisation's life, its total income will be represented by net cash flows generated. However, because of the requirement to prepare periodic financial statements, it is necessary to break up an organisation's operating cycle into artificial periods. Therefore, at each reporting date, an organisation will have entered into a number of incomplete transactions, e.g. a product has been delivered or service rendered for which payment has not yet been received. As a result, the important questions to be answered with respect to revenue recognition revolve around how to allocate the effects of incomplete transactions between the periods for reporting purposes, rather than simply letting them fall into the periods in which cash is received or paid.

The critical event in the operating cycle of a business is the point at which most or all of the uncertainty surrounding a transaction is removed. This is usually when the goods or services are delivered, and is (normally) the point at which revenue is recognised. However, the critical event could occur at other times in the operating cycle, depending on the circumstances. The points in the operating cycle are outlined in Table 1.

In Ireland and Britain, attempts have been made to address revenue recognition in, for example, SSAP 2 *Disclosure of Accounting Policies*, which has been replaced by FRS 18 *Accounting Policies*, Chapter Five of the *Statement of Principles for Financial Reporting* (the UK GAAP equivalent of the *Conceptual Framework for Financial Reporting 2010*) and FRS 5 *Reporting the Substance of Transactions*. However, they arguably only offer limited guidance, and thus reliance has to be placed on international pronouncements, such as IAS 18 *Revenue*.

The growing complexity and diversity of business activity has resulted in a variety of forms of revenue-earning transactions that were never considered when the 'point of sale' was established as the general rule for revenue recognition. As we move further towards a statement of financial position based on the fair value approach to revenue recognition, long-established principles centred on accruals and prudence may no longer be appropriate. In addition, with the prospect of a single statement of financial performance, there is the possibility that traditional concepts of revenue resulting from success, or otherwise, of selling goods and services may become meshed with newer concepts of holding gains and losses.

Table 1: Revenue Recognition and the Operating Cycle

Different Points in Revenue Operating Cycle	Criteria for Revenue Recognition	Examples of Practical Application
Placing of an order by a customer prior to manufacture	Little or no uncertainty regarding the final outcome of the contract. However, in most cases, as there is likely to be uncertainty regarding the final outcome of such contracts it would generally not be prudent to recognise revenue at this point.	In some circumstances revenue may be recognised at this point in the case of long-term construction contracts (see Chapter 12 of *Connolly*).
During production	If revenues accrue over time, and no significant uncertainty exists as to measurability or collectability, then revenue may be recognised.	This may apply to interest, dividends and royalties as the right to receive typically accrues on a time basis (even though the actual payment may only occur annually).
	If a contract of sale has been entered into and future costs can be estimated with reasonable certainty then revenue recognition may be possible.	This may apply to long-term construction contracts where the percentage of completion method is adopted (see Chapter 12 of *Connolly*).

At the completion of production	This is nearing the point where most of the uncertainties in the operating cycle in a business are resolved. For revenue to be recognised, there should be a ready market for the commodity, together with a determinable and stable market price. In addition, the selling and marketing costs involved should be insignificant. In most cases, recognition is usually delayed until delivery.	Certain precious metals and commodities.
At the time of sale (but before delivery)	The goods must have already been acquired or manufactured, and be capable of immediate delivery. The selling price should be established and all material-related expenses, including delivery, ascertained. No significant uncertainties should remain (i.e. cash collection should be reasonably certain, with the likelihood of goods being returned low).	Certain sales of goods (e.g. bill and hold sales). Property sales where there is an irrevocable contract.
On delivery	In this case, while the criteria for recognition before delivery were not met, no significant uncertainties now remain. In the vast majority of cases this is the point at which revenue is recognised.	This is the point at which revenue is recognised for most goods and services. Property sales where there is doubt that the sale will be completed.
Subsequent to delivery	This point in the cycle may be appropriate where there was significant uncertainty regarding collectability at the time of delivery or, at the time of sale, it was not possible to value the consideration with sufficient accuracy.	Sales where right of return exist or goods shipped subject to conditions (e.g. installation, inspection or maintenance).
On an apportionment basis (revenue allocation approach)	Where the revenue represents the supply of initial and subsequent goods or services.	Franchise fees or the sale of goods with an after-sales service.

Coffee – 14 February 2012 – Response

Reasons include:

1. Part of the plan to develop a strong, integrated pan-European capital market. Currently, the markets are nationally regulated with numerous cross-border restrictions that prevent the free flow of capital within Europe.
2. Weaknesses in many European national GAAPs.
3. Many European accounting standard setters are volunteer professional committees and lack the resources to do the kind of work that the IASB is doing.
4. IFRSs are widely regarded as more rigorous than many European national GAAPs. There are important benefits to capital markets of rigorous financial reporting standards.
5. Comparability of the financial statements of European companies with those of companies in other parts of the world, therefore helping European companies raise capital outside of Europe.

Coffee – 17 March 2012 – Response

1. The fact that the *IFRS Framework* involves judgement does not mean that it should be abandoned.
2. The guidance developed by the interpretations committee would be *ad hoc* – that is, developed case by case without the foundation of the *IFRS Framework* to look to. The standards themselves would suffer from the same problem if there were no *Framework*.
3. The *IFRS Framework* provides guidance and direction to the standard setters, and therefore will lead to consistency among the standards.
4. But it is a set of concepts. It provides a boundary for the exercise of judgement by the standard-setter and the interpretive body.

Coffee – 11 April 2012 – Response

1. Conservatism is not a concept in the *IFRS Framework*.
2. Conservatism is intentional bias – downward bias in recognising profits and assets and an upward bias in recognising expenses and liabilities.
3. Amounts reported in financial statements should not be biased. Biased numbers do not help investors to decide whether to put resources into an enterprise and at what price.
4. Prudence is different from conservatism. Prudence is the inclusion of a degree of caution in the exercise of the judgements needed in making the estimates required under conditions of uncertainty, such that assets or income are not overstated and liabilities or expenses are not understated. Prudence is consistent with the *IFRS Framework*, but conservatism is not.

Coffee – 30 April 2012 – Response

1. The *IFRS Framework* identifies the principal classes of users of general purpose financial statements as:
   - present and potential investors;
   - lenders;
   - suppliers and other trade payables;
   - employees;
   - customers;
   - governments and their agencies; and
   - the general public.
2. All of these categories of users rely on financial statements to help them in making various kinds of economic and public policy decisions. Investors need to decide whether to buy, sell, or hold shares. Lenders need to decide whether to lend and at what price. Suppliers need to decide whether to extend credit. Employees need to make rational career decisions. And so on. Information is decision-useful if it helps these people make their decisions.
3. Because investors are providers of risk capital to the enterprise, financial statements that meet their needs will also meet most of the general financial information needs of the other classes of users. Common to all of these user groups is their interest in the ability of an enterprise to generate cash and cash equivalents and of the timing and certainty of those future cash flows. Therefore, the *IFRS Framework* regards investors as the primary, overriding user group.
4. The *IFRS Framework* notes that financial statements cannot provide all the information that users may need to make economic decisions. For one thing, financial statements show the financial effects of past events and transactions, whereas the decisions that most users of financial statements have to make relate to the future. Further, financial statements provide only a limited amount of the non-financial information needed by users of financial statements.
5. Financial statements cannot meet all of the diverse information needs of these user groups. However, there are information needs that are common to all users, and general purpose financial statements focus on meeting those needs.
6. While the concepts in the *IFRS Framework* are likely to lead to information that is useful to the management of a business enterprise in running the business, the *Framework* does not purport to address their information needs. The same can be said for the International Financial Reporting Standards and Interpretations themselves.

Coffee – 20 May 2012 – Response

Accounting profit is defined in IAS 12 *Income Taxes* (paragraph 5) as 'net profit or loss for a period before deducting tax expense', net profit or loss being the excess (or deficiency) of revenues less expenses for that period. Such revenues and expenses would be determined and recognised in accordance with accounting standards and the conceptual *IFRS Framework*. Taxable profit is defined in the same paragraph as 'the profit for a period, determined in accordance with the rules established by the taxation authorities, upon which income taxes are payable'. Taxable profit is the excess of taxable income over taxation deductions allowable against that income. Thus, accounting profit and taxable profit – because they are determined by different principles and rules – are unlikely to be the same figure in any one period. Income tax expense cannot be determined by simply multiplying the accounting profit by the applicable taxation rate. Instead, accounting for income taxes involves identifying and accounting for the differences between accounting profit and taxable profit. These differences arise from a number of common transactions and may be either permanent or temporary in nature.

Coffee – 14 June 2012 – Response

When a new tax rate (or rule) is enacted or substantively enacted, not only should the new rate (rule) be applied in calculating the current tax liability and adjustments to deferred tax accounts during the year, but they should also be applied to the deferred amounts recognised in prior years. A journal adjustment must be passed to increase or reduce the carrying amounts of deferred tax assets and liabilities to reflect the new value of future taxable or deductible amounts. IAS 12 *Income Taxes* (paragraph 60) requires that the net amount arising from the restatement of deferred tax balances be recognised in the statement of comprehensive income except to the extent that the deferred tax amounts relate to items previously charged or credited to equity.

Failing to adjust for the changes will result in deferred tax assets and liabilities being overstated or understated with respect to the reversal of tax effects.

Coffee – 14 July 2012 – Response

The objective of a statement of financial position is to provide information about an entity's financial position, by summarising the entity's assets, liabilities and equity. It thus provides the basic information for evaluating an entity's capital structure and analysing its liquidity, solvency and financial flexibility and also provides a basis for computing rates of return and measures of solvency and liquidity.

The major limitations of a statement of financial position as a source of information about an entity's financial position are:
1. The optional measurement of certain assets, such as property, plant and equipment at historical cost or depreciated historical cost (where the asset has a limited life) rather than current value. Hence there may be a lack of comparability between the statement of financial position of one entity and the statement of financial position of another. Further, the use of cost/depreciated cost as the basis of measurement leads to the statement of financial position not giving a view of the current value of recognised assets.
2. The mandatory omission of intangible self-generated assets (such as brand names and mastheads and goodwill) from the statement of financial position as required by IAS 38 *Intangible Assets*.

3. The omission of various rights and obligations (such as non-cancellable operating leases) from the statement of financial position. This is particularly important as their omission results in liabilities and assets not being reported in the statement of financial position and thus the reported leverage of the entity is inaccurate.
4. Because of the above, the statement of financial position of an entity does not purport to present a total picture of the real worth of the entity, nor does it purport to report all assets controlled by the entity and all the obligations of the entity.

Coffee – 4 August 2012 – Response

Classification of expenses by nature is according to their type of expense (such as, materials used, transport costs, employee benefits, depreciation, electricity, advertising costs, finance costs). Classification by function is according to the activity involved (such as, cost of sales, selling and distribution costs, administration, and finance costs).

For a manufacturer, distributor or retailer, classification of expenses by function will ordinarily be considered more relevant to a user as a prime measure of performance is the percentage of gross margin on sales and this can only be determined if cost of sales is reported. Further, for such entities, performance is better measured if costs by function can be expressed as a percentage of sales (for example, percentage of selling and distribution costs to sales). This is despite the fact that judgement is necessary in allocating expenses to the various functions and so comparability between entities may be variable. However, for an individual entity consistency should exist between periods so that expense patterns can be analysed over a number of periods.

In the case of a finance company and certain service companies, classification by nature of expense will often provide more relevant information, as for such companies key indicators of performance are the margin of interest earned over interest paid, and the level of key expenses such as employee costs and rent as a percentage of revenue.

Coffee – 3 September 2012 – Response

Details of accounting policies are important for ensuring the understandability of financial statements to general users of financial statements for the following reasons:
1. Various options exist in certain IFRSs (such as the option to revalue property, plant and equipment as an alternative to using historical costs) and therefore it is essential that the summary of accounting policies identifies which options have been adopted (where relevant); and
2. Under IFRSs various assets of an entity (such as internally generated brand names and self-generated goodwill) and rights and obligations (such as non-cancellable operating leases) are not recognised in an entity's statement of financial position. The summary of accounting policies helps ensure users of financial statements are aware of these omissions.

Coffee – 10 October 2012 – Response

Statement of Financial Position Account:	Statement of Financial Position Caption:	Statement of Financial Position Classification:
Trade receivables	Trade and other receivables	Current assets
Work in progress	Inventories	Current assets
Trade payables	Trade and other payables	Current liability
Prepayments	Other current assets	Current assets
Property	Property, plant and equipment	Non-current assets
Goodwill	Intangible assets	Non-current assets
Debentures outstanding	Financial liabilities or a separate caption 'borrowings'	Current or non-current liabilities depending on their repayment period
Preference share capital	Issued capital or liabilities depending on whether the instruments meet the definition of a liability or constitute equity	Equity or if they constitute a liability current or non-current liabilities depending on the period of redemption
Unearned revenue	Other liabilities or a separate caption if material	Current or non-current liabilities depending on the applicable period of the unearned revenue
Accrued salaries	Trade and other payables	Current liabilities
Trading securities held	Financial assets (captioned as 'trading securities held')	Current assets
Share capital	Share capital	Equity
Dividends payable	Provisions or separate caption 'dividends payable'	Current liability

Coffee – 1 November 2012 – Response

For many of us, the move to international accounting and financial reporting standards initially meant getting used to new terminology, principles and practices. For example, in 2007, the IASB issued a revised IAS 1. While the changes were relatively minor, they represented the first step in the IASB's comprehensive project on reporting financial information. Changes in terminology at this point included:

- a statement of financial position (previously 'balance sheet');
- a statement of comprehensive income (previously 'income statement'); and
- a statement of cash flows (previously 'cash flow statement').

While much of the changes were arguably quite subtle and even superficial, from a practical perspective, two important changes were:

1. Dividends paid were no longer included in the statement of comprehensive income (see further below, subsequently renamed statement of profit or loss and other comprehensive income): they are an appropriation and therefore should be shown in the statement of changes in equity. Proposed dividends are not accrued until approved by shareholders at the AGM in accordance with IAS 10 *Events After the Reporting Period*.
2. Extraordinary items were banned and it is a decision for the company to highlight/ separately disclose 'material' items (previously referred to as 'exceptional items'). IAS 1 makes no reference to 'super exceptional' items.

In June 2011, the IASB issued further amendments to IAS 1 *Presentation of Financial Statements*. These included the adoption of the title 'Statement of Profit or Loss and Other Comprehensive Income' (SPLOCI); although IAS 1 still permits the use of other titles (e.g. statement of comprehensive income).

Ethical Dilemma – Response

The retiring partner will need to have regard to any conditions in his partnership agreement as to restrictions on taking up employment/appointment as an officer of a company on leaving the partnership. If he would not be in breach of contract by taking up the non-executive role then he is free to do so. Under APB Ethical Standard 2, "audit firms should establish policies and procedures that require all partners in the audit firm to notify the firm of any situation involving their potential employment with any audit client of the firm" (ES 2, paragraph 40). However, if he chooses to accept the appointment, the partnership will have to consider withdrawing from the audit since, in the circumstances, it is unlikely that sufficient safeguards could be put in place.

Coffee – 28 November 2012 – Response

Financial statements should be presented at least annually and should be issued on a timely basis to be useful to users. A complete set of financial statements includes: a statement of financial position; a statement of profit or loss and other comprehensive income; a statement of changes in equity; a statement of cash flows; and accounting policies and explanatory notes. The statement of changes in equity is the frequently ignored and misunderstood member of the financial statements family.

This component of a set of financial statements is based upon the principle that changes in an enterprise's equity between two reporting dates reflect the increase or decrease in its net assets or wealth during the period. This information is useful to users as such changes, excluding changes resulting from transactions with shareholders (e.g. capital injections and dividends), represent the total gains and losses generated by the enterprise in that period.

As discussed previously with respect to the statement of profit or loss and other comprehensive income, under the revised IAS 1, the components that make up an entity's comprehensive income must *not* be shown in the statement of changes in equity. While this statement includes the total amount of comprehensive income, its main purpose is to show the amounts of transactions with owners (e.g. share issues and dividends) and to provide a reconciliation of the opening and closing balance of each class of equity and reserve. An example is presented below:

X Limited
STATEMENT OF CHANGES IN EQUITY
for the Year Ended 31 December 2012

	Share capital €/£	Other reserves €/£	Retained earnings €/£	Total €/£
Opening balance	x	x	x	x
Changes in accounting policy	—	—	x	x
Restated balance	x	x	x	x
Changes in equity for the year				
Total comprehensive income		x	x	x
Dividends			(x)	(x)
Issue of share capital	x	—	—	x
Total changes in equity	x	x	x	x
Closing balance	x	x	x	x

MY COMPANY LIMITED
FINANCIAL STATEMENTS
For the Year Ended 31 December 2012

FILE INDEX

Section

- A.   Financial Statements
- B.   Final Trial Balance
- C.   Adjusting Journal Entries
- D.   End of Year Adjustments
- E.   Draft Trial Balance
- F.   Statement of Profit or Loss and Other Comprehensive Income Lead Schedule
- G.   Statement of Financial Position Lead Schedules
- H.   Statement of Cash Flows Lead Schedule

SECTION A: FINANCIAL STATEMENTS

My Company Limited
Statement of Profit or Loss and Other Comprehensive Income
Year ended 31 December 2012

	Note	31 December 2012 €/£	31 December 2012 €/£	31 December 2011 €/£	31 December 2011 €/£
Revenue			1,637,600		1,310,300
Cost of Sales:					
Opening inventory		77,800		60,000	
Purchases		423,045		396,200	
Closing inventory		(91,255)		(77,800)	
		409,590		378,400	
Manufacturing staff costs		420,250		383,100	
Depreciation plant and machinery		23,100		22,600	
Loss on disposal of equipment		2,000	(854,940)	–	(784,100)
Gross Profit			782,660		526,200
Distribution Costs:					
Staff costs		290,000		256,300	
Depreciation fixtures and fittings		20,580	(310,580)	19,780	(276,080)
Administrative Expenses:					
Staff costs		34,100		20,000	
Depreciation freehold properties		12,820		8,400	
Amortisation software licences		10,000		10,000	
Other		128,960	(185,880)	117,400	(155,800)
Operating Profit			286,200		94,320
Finance cost			(36,829)		(37,610)
Profit before tax			249,371		56,710
Income tax expense			(50,000)		(11,000)
Profit after tax			199,371		45,710
Other comprehensive income:					
Items that will not be reclassified into profit or loss – revaluation			21,000		–
Total comprehensive income			220,371		45,710

My Company Limited
STATEMENT OF FINANCIAL POSITION
31 December 2012

	Note	31 December 2012 €/£	31 December 2012 €/£	31 December 2011 €/£	31 December 2011 €/£
ASSETS					
Non-current Assets					
Freehold properties			428,039		219,859
Plant and equipment			120,645		132,745
Fixtures and fittings			31,941		48,521
			580,625		401,125
Intangible – software licences			50,000		60,000
			630,625		461,125
Current Assets					
Inventory – Raw materials		55,395		40,200	
– Work in progress		17,110		18,100	
– Finished goods		18,750		19,500	
Trade receivables		99,940		95,950	
Other receivables		3,400		2,700	
Prepayments		1,500		1,400	
Bank and cash		10,323	206,418	10,254	188,104
			837,043		649,229
EQUITY AND LIABILITIES					
Capital and Reserves					
€/£1 ordinary shares			100,000		100,000
Revaluation reserve			45,525		24,525
Retained earnings			564,285		364,914
			709,810		489,439
Non-current Liabilities					
Provision for liabilities and charges			50,000		35,000
Current Liabilities					
Trade payables		20,533		19,473	
Other payables		54,700		103,417	
Accruals		2,000	77,233	1,900	124,790
			837,043		649,229

My Company Limited
Statement of Cash Flows
Year ended 31 December 2012

	Note	31 December 2012 €/£	31 December 2011 €/£
Net cash flow from operating activities		217,069	183,461
Cash flows from investing activities		(217,000)	(187,961)
Cash flows from financing activities		–	5,000
Net increase in cash and cash equivalents		69	500
Cash and cash equivalents at start of year		10,254	9,754
Cash and cash equivalents at end of year		10,323	10,254

My Company Limited
Statement of Changes in Equity
Year ended 31 December 2012

	Share capital €/£	Revaluation reserve €/£	Retained earnings €/£	Total €/£
At 1 January 2012	100,000	24,525	364,914	489,439
Changes in equity for the year:				
Recognised in total comprehensive income	–	21,000	199,371	220,371
At 31 December 2012	100,000	45,525	564,285	709,810

My Company Limited
Notes to the Financial Statements
Year ended 31 December 2012
(Extract)

1. **Statement of Accounting Policies**

    The following accounting policies have been applied consistently in dealing with items which are considered material in relation to the accounts.

    1.1 **Basis of Accounting**

    These financial statements have been prepared under the historical cost convention, modified to include the revaluation of non-current assets.

    1.2 **Intangible Assets**

    These comprise the value of capitalised operational software licences. The value of licences is amortised over their expected useful lives.

    1.3 **Property, Plant and Equipment, and Fixtures and Fittings**

    Title to the freehold properties shown in the accounts is held by My Company Limited. Freehold properties have been included on the basis of professional valuations.

    The minimum level for capitalisation of property, plant and equipment, and fixtures and fittings is €/£500.

    1.4 **Depreciation**

    Depreciation is provided at rates calculated to write off the valuation of freehold properties, plant and equipment, and fixtures and fittings by equal instalments over their estimated useful lives as follows:

Freehold properties	50 years
Plant and equipment	10 years
Fixtures and fittings	5 years

    1.5 **Inventory and Work-in-progress**

    Inventory and work-in-progress are valued as follows:
    - (i) finished goods and goods for resale are valued at the lower of cost and net realisable value; and
    - (ii) work-in-progress is valued at the lower of cost, including appropriate overheads, and net realisable value.

    1.6 **Sales Revenue**

    Sales revenue is shown net of value added tax.

    1.7 **Foreign Exchange**

    Revenue and expenditure incurred in foreign currencies which are not covered by a forward contract are translated at the rate of exchange ruling on the date of the transaction. Balances held in foreign currencies not covered by forward contracts are translated at the rate of exchange ruling at the reporting date. Where there are related forward contracts, the rate of exchange specified in the contract is used.

2. **Operating Income**

An analysis of sales revenue by product type and geographical region is as follows:

	2012	2011
	€/£	€/£

3. **Staff Numbers and Costs**

The average number of whole-time equivalent persons employed (including senior management) during the year was as follows:

	2012	2011
Activity 1	3	3
Activity 2	13	11
Activity 3	5	5
Activity 4	2	3
	23	22

[*Should be presented on a suitable and consistent basis, for example by product/service or geographical area.*]

The aggregate payroll costs of these persons were as follows:

	2012	2011
	€/£	€/£
Wages and Salaries		
Social Security costs		
Other Pension costs		

For the year ended 31 December 2012, the total remuneration of the Chairman who was also the highest paid senior member of staff, including bonuses, taxable value of benefits and pension contributions was €/£xxx,xxx.

The number of other employees, including senior operational staff, whose remuneration excluding pension contributions exceeded €/£40,000 was as follows:

€/£40,000 – €/£49,999	2
€/£50,000 – €/£59,999	0
€/£60,000 – €/£69,999	1
€/£70,000 – €/£79,999	1

MCL's Management Board comprises both senior operational management and external appointees. The remuneration of senior management is included above. The aggregate cost of the external Board appointments in the period was €/£xxx,xxx and external Board appointees' remuneration excluding pension contributions was in the following ranges:

| €/£0 – €/£4,999 | 5 |
| €/£5,000 – €/£9,999 | 1 |

4. Profit After Tax

	2012 €/£	2011 €/£
Profit after tax is arrived at after charging:		
Hire of plant and machinery	17,500	16,200
Auditors' remuneration	24,100	23,000
Expenditure on staff training and development	13,300	14,100

5. Statement of Cash Flows

	2012 €/£	2011 €/£
Net cash flow from operating activities		
Profit before tax	249,371	
Depreciation	56,500	
Amortisation	10,000	
Interest charge	36,829	
Loss on disposal of equipment	2,000	
Increase in inventory	(13,455)	
Increase in trade receivables	(3,990)	
Increase in other receivables	(700)	
Increase in prepayments	(100)	
Increase in trade payables	1,060	
Increase in accruals	100	
Increase in provisions	15,000	
Interest paid	(36,829)	
Tax paid	(98,717)	
	217,069	
Cash flows from investing activities		
Purchase of non-current assets	(219,000)	
Proceeds from disposal of equipment	2,000	
	(217,000)	

6. Intangible Non-current Assets

Certain operational software licences are held by MCL. A valuation of these licences was undertaken by AA Consultants on 1 January 2012.

	€/£
Cost or Valuation:	
At 1 January 2012	80,000
Additions	-
At 31 December 2012	80,000
Amortisation:	
At 1 January 2012	20,000
Provided during year	10,000
At 31 December 2012	30,000
Net Book Value:	
At 31 December 2012	50,000
At 31 December 2011	60,000

7. **Property, Plant and Equipment, and Fixtures and Fittings:**

	Freehold Properties €/£	Plant and Equipment €/£	Fixtures and Fittings €/£	Total €/£
Cost/Valuation:				
At 1 January 2012	420,000	226,000	98,900	744,900
Additions	200,000	15,000	4,000	219,000
Disposals	-	(10,000)	-	(10,000)
Revaluation	21,000	-	-	21,000
At 31 December 2012	641,000	231,000	102,900	974,900
Depreciation:				
At 1 January 2012	200,141	93,255	50,379	343,775
Charged in year	12,820	23,100	20,580	56,500
On disposals	-	(6,000)	-	(6,000)
At 31 December 2012	212,961	110,355	70,959	394,275
Carrying Value:				
At 31 December 2012	428,039	120,645	31,941	580,625
At 31 December 2011	219,859	132,745	48,521	401,125

Freehold properties were revalued on 31 December 2012 by Anybody, Chartered Surveyors, on the basis of open market value for existing use.

8. **Inventory and work-in-progress**

	2012 €/£	2011 €/£
Raw materials	55,395	40,200
Work-in-progress	17,110	18,100
Finished goods	18,750	19,500
	91,255	77,800

9. **Receivables**

	2012 €/£	2011 €/£
Amounts falling due within one year:		
Trade receivables	105,200	101,000
Allowance for irrecoverable debts	(5,260)	(5,050)
	99,940	95,950
Other receivables – VAT	3,400	2,700
Prepayments – lease of plant and machinery	1,500	1,400
	104,840	100,050

There are no receivables falling due over one year.

10. Cash at Bank and in Hand

	2012 €/£	2011 €/£
Bank	10,223	10,154
Cash-in-hand	100	100
	10,323	10,254

11. Payables

	2012 €/£	2011 €/£
Trade payables	20,533	19,473
Other payables – income tax	54,700	103,417
Accruals	2,000	1,900
	77,233	124,790

12. Provisions for Liabilities and Charges

	Early retirement and pension costs €/£
Balance at 1 January 2012	35,000
Provision during year	15,000
Balance at 31 December 2012	50,000

See also notes 13 and 14.

13. Pensions

Present and past employees are covered by the provisions of the MCL Pension Scheme which is a non-contributory and non-funded defined benefit scheme. For 2012, contributions of €/£158,000 were paid into the Scheme at rates determined by the Actuary. For 2012, these rates were in the range 11–14% of pensionable pay for non-industrial staff and 12% for industrial staff.

14. Early retirement costs

MCL is required to pay the pensions of employees who retire early until they reach normal pensionable age. The total pension liability arising from reorganisation and from early retirement in previous years, up to the normal retirement age of each employee, was charged as a provision in 2011.

15. **Capital Commitments**

    Capital commitments (excluding VAT) for which no provision has been made in these accounts were as follows:

	2012 €/£	2011 €/£
Contracted	54,000	70,200
Authorised but not contracted	63,000	15,000

16. **Contingent Liabilities**

    There were no contingent liabilities at 31 December 2012.

17. **Events After the Reporting Period**

    On 23 January 2013, MCL made a conditional agreement to sell one of its freehold properties to ABC Developers Ltd for a consideration of €/£500,000. The net asset value of the property is approximately €/£120,000. Legal completion is expected to take place on 14 June 2013.

SECTION B: TRIAL BALANCE

My Company Limited
FINAL TRIAL BALANCE
31 December 2012

	€/£ DR	€/£ CR
Purchases of materials	423,045	
Manufacturing staff costs:		
Salaries and wages	310,250	
Social security costs	40,800	
Other pension costs	69,200	
Administrative costs:		
Telephone	7,600	
Heat and light	41,750	
Insurance	15,200	
Hire of plant and machinery	17,500	
Audit	24,100	
Staff training and development	13,300	
Irrecoverable debts	210	
General	9,300	
Depreciation	56,500	
Amortisation	10,000	
Sales		1,637,600
Profit/loss on disposal of equipment	2,000	
Finance charges	36,829	
Administrative staff costs:		
Salaries and wages	26,500	
Social security costs	3,500	
Other pension costs	4,100	
Distribution staff costs:		
Salaries and wages	239,000	
Social security costs	44,000	
Other pension costs	7,000	
Income tax	50,000	
Intangible non-current assets:		
Software licences – Cost at 1.1.12	80,000	
Software licences – Amortisation at 1.1.12		20,000
– Amortisation charge		10,000

		€/£ DR	€/£ CR
Property, plant and equipment, and fixtures and fittings:			
Freehold properties	– Cost/valuation at 1.1.12	420,000	
	– Additions	200,000	
	– Revaluation	21,000	
Freehold properties	– Depreciation at 1.1.12		200,141
	– Charge for year		12,820
Plant and equipment	– Cost at 1.1.12	226,000	
	– Additions	15,000	
	– Disposals		10,000
Plant and equipment	– Depreciation at 1.1.12		93,255
	– On disposals	6,000	
	– Charge for year		23,100
Fixtures and fittings	– Cost at 1.1.12	98,900	
	– Additions	4,000	
Fixtures and fittings	– Depreciation at 1.1.12		50,379
	– Charge for year		20,580
Inventory:			
Raw materials		55,395	
Work-in-progress		17,110	
Finished goods		18,750	
Receivables:			
Trade		105,200	
Allowance for irrecoverable debts		5,260	
Other receivables		3,400	
Prepayments		1,500	
Cash at bank		10,223	
Cash-in-hand		100	
Current liabilities:			
Trade payables			20,533
Other payables			54,700
Accruals			2,000
Provision for liabilities and charges:			
Early retirement and pension costs			50,000
Revaluation reserve – freehold properties			45,525
€/£1 ordinary shares			100,000
Retained earnings			378,369
		2,734,262	2,734,262

SECTION C: ADJUSTING JOURNAL ENTRIES

My Company Limited
Adjusting Journal Entries (aje)
Year ended 31 December 2012

			DR €/£	CR €/£
1.(a)	DR Electricity Expense		10,300	
	CR Bank No. 1 A/C			10,300

— Being standing order for electricity paid by bank on 24.12.12 not recorded in cash book at year end.

(b)	DR Bank No 1 A/C	10,200	
	CR Trade Receivables		10,200

— Being credit transfer received by bank on 28.12.12 from trade receivable.

2.	DR Software Licence Amortisation SPLOCI–P/L	10,000	
	CR Software Licence Amortisation SFP		10,000

— Being software licence amortisation charge for year ended 31.12.12.

3.	DR Closing Inventory – Raw Materials	10,895	
	CR Closing Inventory – Work-in-progress		1,890
	CR Closing Inventory – Finished goods		2,750
	CR Purchases		6,255

— Being correction to closing inventory valuation at 31 December 2012 following a review of inventory-take working papers.

4.	DR Irrecoverable Debts Expense	210	
	CR Allowance for Irrecoverable Debts		210

— To maintain allowance for irrecoverable debts at 31 December 2012 at 5% of trade receivables at the reporting date.

New provision 5% (115,400 – 10,200)
Increase (5,260 – 5,050)

5.	DR Prepayments	100	
	CR Hire of Plant and Machinery		100

— To properly state prepaid hire charges at 31 December 2012.

6.	DR Purchases	5,500	
	CR Trade Payables		5,500

— Being net adjustments to reconcile trade payables control account at 31 December 2012.

		DR €/£	CR €/£

7. DR Telephone Expense 100
   CR Telephone Accrual 100
   – Being adjustment to properly record telephone accrual at 31 December 2012.

8. DR Depreciation Charge SPLOCI–P/L 56,500
   CR Accumulated Depreciation – FB 50 years 12,820
                                – P & E 10 years 23,100
                                – F & F 5 years 20,580
   – Being depreciation charge for year ended 31 December 2012.

9. DR Income tax expense 50,000
   CR Other Payables – income tax 50,000
   – Being income tax payable for year ended 31 December 2012.

My Company Limited
Bank and Cash

Bank Reconciliation
No. 1 Account
31 December 2012

Cash Book

	€/£		€/£
Balance per TB	10,323	Standing Order (Journal 1)	10,300
Credit Transfer (Journal 2)	10,200	Balance c/d	10,223
	20,523		20,523
Balance b/d	10,223		

Reconciled by:

	€/£
Balance per bank statement at 31.12.12	(590)
Add: Deposits not cleared	11,054
Less: Unpresented cheques	(241)
Balance per cash book	10,223

My Company Limited
Intangible Non-Current Assets
Year ended 31 December 2012

Amortisation of Software Licences:

Per Note 1, the value of licences is amortised on a straight-line basis over 8 years:

	€/£
Value at 1.1.12	80,000
	÷8
Amortisation for year	10,000

My Company Limited
Inventory held
at 31 December 2012

	Raw Materials €/£	Work-in-progress €/£	Finished goods €/£
Preliminary valuation	44,500	19,000	21,500
(a) No adjustment as cost < NRV	–	–	–
(b) Reduction to NRV	(1,300)	–	–
(c) Arithmetic corrected	(1,260)	–	720
(d) Omitted items	4,010	–	–
(e) Transposition error	–	(1,890)	–
(f) Goods omitted	16,380	–	–
(g) Hired item, not inventory	–	–	(3,470)
(h) Samples should be excluded	(2,425)	–	–
(i) Reduce to cost	(1,840)	–	–
(j) Held only on sale or return	(2,670)	–	–
Revised Valuation	55,395	17,110	18,750

My Company Limited
Allowance for Irrecoverable Debts
Year ended 31 December 2012

	€/£
Adjusted trade receivables balance	105,200
Allowance at 5%	5,260
Allowance per draft TB	5,050
Charge for year ended 31 December 2012	210

My Company Limited
PREPAYMENTS
Year ended 31 December 2012

The prepayment at 31 December 2011 was €/£1,400

i.e. $\dfrac{4,200}{3}$

The prepayment at 31 December 2012 was €/£1,500

i.e. $\dfrac{4,500}{3}$

The charge for year ended 31 December 2012 is:

1 January – 31 January 2012	1,400
1 February – 30 April 2012	4,300
1 May – 31 July 2012	4,400
1 August – 31 October 2012	4,400
1 November – 31 December 2012	3,000
	17,500
Charge per draft TB	17,600
Increase prepayment	100

My Company Limited
TRADE PAYABLES
Year ended 31 December 2012

Looking first at the Payables Control Account. The errors affecting the control account are (c) and (d).

For error (c) Mr Able's invoice had not been recorded in the Purchases Day Book so it would not have been included in the total debited to purchases and credited to the payables control a/c (it will also not be in his individual ledger a/c). To correct the control account we need to:

DR	Purchases A/C	€/£7,000	
CR	Payables Control A/C		€/£7,000

For error (d) if the invoice was recorded twice the total posted to the payables control a/c would be too much by the amount of the invoice. We need to reverse this entry:

DR	Payables Control A/C	€/£1,500	
CR	Purchases A/C		€/£1,500

(Also, it will have been posted to Mr Will's individual ledger account twice.)

Showing these adjustments in the Payables Control Account:

Payables Control Account

	€/£		€/£
		Balance b/d	15,033
		Invoice not recorded (c)	7000
Invoice recorded twice (d)	1,500		
Balance c/d	20,533		
	22,033		22,033
		Balance b/d	20,533

Errors affecting the list of balances are (a), (b), (c) and (d):

Error (a) A credit balance was missed out so should now be added in.

Error (b) Mr Can's account needs to be credited with €/£2,300 to record the invoice.

Error (c) Mr Able's account needs to be credited with €/£7,000 to record the invoice.

Error (d) Mr Will's account has two credit entries relating to the same invoice of €/£1,500. One of these needs to be reversed so we must debit his account with €/£1,500.

Showing these adjustments to the original list of balances:

	€/£
Original total of list of balances	9,333
Credit balance omitted (a)	3,400
Invoice not recorded (Mr Can) (b)	2,300
Invoice not recorded (Mr Able) (c)	7,000
Invoice recorded twice (Mr Will) (d)	(1,500)
Corrected total of list of balances	20,533

This is now equal to the control account balance.

Note, if we had not discovered error (d) the control account would still have balanced with the total of the list of balances since equal errors were made to both accounts. Likewise, error (c) caused both the control account and list of balances to be wrong by an equal amount. In these cases a business will use 'statements' sent to them by their creditors to act as a check on each individual account balance to help detect errors. A statement is a summary of all the invoices issued to a business by its supplier.

My Company Limited
Accruals
Year ended 31 December 2012

The statement of profit or loss and other comprehensive income should be charged with the cost of the telephone calls made from 1 January 2012 to 31 December 2012.

This will be:

	€/£
1 January 2012 – 31 March 2012	1,800
1 April 2012 – 30 June 2012	1,600
1 July 2012 – 31 September 2012	2,200
1 October 2012 – 31 December 2012	2,000
	7,600

As at 31 December 2012, MCL had not paid for the telephone calls that it had made in the last quarter but it is an expense of the year to 31 December 2012 and so must be accrued. The accrual is therefore €/£2,000.

My Company Limited
Property, Plant and Equipment, and Fixtures and Fittings
Year ended 31 December 2012

Depreciation:

	Freehold properties €/£	Plant and equipment €/£	Fixtures and fittings €/£
Cost/valuation at 31 December 2012	641,000	231,000	102,900
Estimated useful lives (Years)	50	10	5
Depreciation for year	12,820	23,100	20,580

Depreciation should be included under the statutory headings as follows:

Freehold properties – administration expenses
Plant and equipment – cost of sales
Fixtures and fittings – distribution costs.

Note:

1. As freehold properties are recorded at valuation, MCL has the option of transferring an amount from the revaluation reserve to retained earnings to offset the additional depreciation. This has not been done in this case.
2. The loss on disposal of equipment should be included within 'cost of sales'. If the loss is considered 'material', it should be disclosed separately within cost of sales, either on the face of the statement of profit or loss and other comprehensive income or in the notes to the financial statements.

SECTION D: END OF YEAR ADJUSTMENTS

My Company Limited
END OF YEAR ADJUSTMENTS
31 December 2012

1. The trial balance shows a debit balance of €/£10,323 at 31 December 2012, whereas the bank statement indicates that MCL is overdrawn by €/£590.

   Following an examination of MCL's records and the bank statement for the period since the last reconciliation, a number of items were noted:

   (a) a standing order for electricity of €/£10,300 had been paid by the bank on 24 December 2012 but no entry had been made in the cash book;

   (b) a credit transfer of €/£10,200 had been received by the bank on 28 December 2012 in settlement of one of MCL's customer accounts. No entry had been made for this in the cash book;

   (c) cheques from customers totalling €/£11,054 were entered in the cash book on 31 December 2012 but did not clear the bank until 1 January 2013;

   (d) cheques issued by MCL to pay trade payables on 29 December 2012 totalling €/£241 did not appear on the bank statement until February 2013.

2. Amortisation of software licences for year ended 31 December 2009 has not yet been provided.

3. After inventory taking for the year ended 31 December 2012 had taken place, the closing inventory of MCL was valued as follows:

	€/£
Raw materials	44,500
Work-in-progress	19,000
Finished goods	21,500
	85,000

   Following a detailed review of the inventory take working papers and discussions with staff, the facts noted below were discovered.

   (a) Some finished goods stored outside had been included at their normal cost price of €/£5,700. They had, however, deteriorated and would require an estimated €/£1,200 to be spent to restore them to their original condition, after which they could be sold for €/£8,000.

   (b) Some raw materials had been damaged and were now unusable. They could, however, be sold for €/£1,100 as spares after repairs estimated at €/£400 had been carried out. They had originally cost €/£2,000.

   (c) One inventory sheet used to record raw materials had been over-added by €/£1,260 and another recording finished goods under-added by €/£720.

   (d) MCL has received raw materials costing €/£4,010 during the last week of December 2012 but, because the invoices did not arrive until February 2013, they have not been included in inventory.

(e) An inventory sheet total of €/£12,340 for work-in-progress has been transferred to a summary sheet as €/£14,230.
(f) Invoices totalling €/£16,380 arrived during the last week of December 2012 (and were included in purchases and payables) but, because of transport delays, the goods did not arrive until late February 2013 and were not included in closing inventory.
(g) Portable generators on hire from another company at a charge of €/£3,470 were included, at this figure, in the inventory of finished goods.
(h) Free samples sent to MCL by various suppliers had been included in the raw materials inventory at the catalogue price of €/£2,425.
(i) Goods costing €/£4,180 sent to customers on a sale or return basis had been included in raw materials inventory by MCL at their selling price of €/£6,020.
(j) Goods sent on a sale or return basis to MCL had been included in the raw materials inventory at the amount payable (€/£2,670) if retained. No decision to retain these items had been made.

4. It is company policy to maintain the allowance for irrecoverable debts at an amount which is equal to 5% of trade receivables at the reporting date.

5. MCL leases certain plant and machinery and pays for them in advance each quarter. During the year ended 31 December 2012, MCL made the following payments in respect of the plant and machinery:

Date Paid	Amount	For Quarter Ending
1.11.11	€/£4,200	31.1.12
1.2.12	€/£4,300	30.4.12
1.5.12	€/£4,400	31.7.12
1.8.12	€/£4,400	31.10.12
1.11.12	€/£4,500	31.1.13

All payments made in year ended 31 December 2012 have been charged in full to the statement of comprehensive income.

6. The balance on the Trade Payables Account at 31 December 2012 was €/£15,033. The balances on the individual accounts in the Payables Ledger were extracted and totalled €/£9,333.

A detailed review of the information highlighted the following:

(a) a credit balance of €/£3,400 had been omitted from the list of balances;
(b) no entry had been made to Mr Can's individual ledger account in respect of an invoice for €/£2,300 which was correctly recorded in the Purchases Day Book;
(c) an invoice from Mr Able for €/£7,000 had not been recorded in the Purchases Day Book;
(d) an invoice from Mr Will for €/£1,500 had been recorded twice in error in the Purchases Day Book.

7. MCL receives its telephone bills quarterly just after the end of each quarter has elapsed. It received the following bills during the last year which it paid on the dates shown.

For Telephone From — To	Amount €/£	Date bill received	Date bill paid
1 Oct 2011 – 31 Dec 2011	1,900	10 Jan 2012	29 Jan 2012
1 Jan 2012 – 31 Mar 2012	1,800	10 Apr 2012	1 May 2012
1 Apr 2012 – 30 Jun 2012	1,600	9 Jul 2012	31 Jul 2012
1 Jul 2012 – 30 Sept 2012	2,200	12 Oct 2012	1 Nov 2012
1 Oct 2012 – 31 Dec 2012	2,000	13 Jan 2013	2 Feb 2013

All payments made during year ended 31 December 2012 have been charged to the statement of profit or loss and other comprehensive income in arriving at profit or loss.

8. Depreciation of property, plant and equipment, and fixtures and fittings for the year ended 31 December 2012 has not yet been charged in the financial statements.

9. MCL's tax charge for 2012, which takes into account all relevant items, is €/£50,000.

SECTION E: DRAFT TRIAL BALANCE

My Company Limited
DRAFT TRIAL BALANCE
31 December 2012

		€/£ DR	€/£ CR
Purchases of materials		423,800	
Manufacturing staff costs:			
Salaries and wages		310,250	
Social security costs		40,800	
Other pension costs		69,200	
Administrative costs:			
Telephone		7,500	
Heat and light		31,450	
Insurance		15,200	
Hire of plant and machinery		17,600	
Audit		24,100	
Staff training and development		13,300	
General		9,300	
Sales			1,637,600
Profit/loss on disposal of equipment		2,000	
Finance charges		36,829	
Administrative staff costs:			
Salaries and wages		26,500	
Social security costs		3,500	
Other pension costs		4,100	
Distribution staff costs:			
Salaries and wages		239,000	
Social security costs		44,000	
Other pension costs		7,000	
Intangible non-current assets:			
Software licences	– Cost at 1.1.12	80,000	
Software licences	– Amortisation at 1.1.12		20,000
Property, plant and equipment, and fixtures and fittings:			
Freehold properties	– Cost/valuation at 1.1.12	420,000	
	– Additions	200,000	
	– Revaluation	21,000	
Freehold properties	– Depreciation at 1.1.12		200,141
Plant and equipment	– Cost at 1.1.12	226,000	
	– Additions	15,000	
	– Disposals		10,000
Plant and equipment	– Depreciation at 1.1.12		93,255
	– On disposals	6,000	

SUGGESTED SOLUTIONS TO SECTION THREE – LIMITED COMPANY

		€/£ DR	€/£ CR
Fixtures and fittings	– Cost at 1.1.12	98,900	
	– Additions	4,000	
Fixtures and fittings	– Depreciation at 1.1.12		50,379
Inventory:			
Raw materials		44,500	
Work-in-progress		19,000	
Finished goods		21,500	
Receivables:			
Trade		115,400	
Allowance for irrecoverable debts			5,050
Other receivables		3,400	
Prepayments		1,400	
Cash at bank		10,323	
Cash-in-hand		100	
Current liabilities:			
Trade payables			15,033
Other payables			4,700
Accruals			1,900
Provision for liabilities and charges:			
Early retirement and pension costs			50,000
Revaluation reserve – freehold properties			45,525
€/£1 ordinary shares			100,000
Retained earnings			378,369
		2,611,952	2,611,952

SECTION F: STATEMENT OF PROFIT OR LOSS AND OTHER COMPREHENSIVE INCOME

My Company Limited
STATEMENT OF PROFIT OR LOSS AND OTHER COMPREHENSIVE INCOME
Year ended 31 December 2012

	2012 €/£	2011 €/£
Revenue	1,637,600	1,310,300
Cost of Sales		
Opening inventory	77,800	60,000
Purchases	423,045	396,200
Closing inventory	(91,255)	(77,800)
	409,590	378,400
Manufacturing staff costs	420,250	383,100
Depreciation plant and machinery	23,100	22,600
Loss on disposal of equipment	2,000	-
	854,940	784,100
Distribution Costs		
Staff costs	290,000	256,300
Depreciation fixtures and fittings	20,580	19,780
	310,580	276,080
Administrative Expenses		
Staff costs	34,100	20,000
Depreciation freehold properties	12,820	8,400
Amortisation software licences	10,000	10,000
Other	123,960	117,400
	185,880	155,800
Finance cost	36,829	37,610
Income tax expense	50,000	11,000

SECTION G: STATEMENT OF FINANCIAL POSITION

My Company Limited
INTANGIBLE NON-CURRENT ASSETS
Year ended 31 December 2012

Software Licences	€/£
Cost/Valuation:	
At 1.1.12	80,000
Additions	–
Disposals	–
At 31.12.12	80,000
Amortisation:	
At 1.1.12	20,000
Provided during year	10,000
At 31.12.12	30,000
Net Book Value:	
At 31.12.12	50,000
At 31.12.11	60,000

My Company Limited
PROPERTY, PLANT AND EQUIPMENT, AND FIXTURES AND FITTINGS
Year ended 31 December 2012

	Freehold Properties €/£	Plant and Equipment €/£	Fixtures and Fittings €/£	Total €/£
Cost/Valuation:				
At 1 January 2012	420,000	226,000	98,900	744,900
Additions	200,000	15,000	4,000	219,000
Disposals	–	(10,000)	–	(10,000)
Revaluation	21,000	–	–	21,000
At 31 December 2012	641,000	231,000	102,900	974,900
Depreciation:				
At 1 January 2012	200,141	93,255	50,379	343,775
Charged in year	12,820	23,100	20,580	56,500
On disposals	–	(6,000)	–	(6,000)
At 31 December 2012	212,961	110,355	70,959	394,275
Net Book Value:				
At 31 December 2012	428,039	120,645	31,941	580,625
At 31 December 2011	219,859	132,745	48,521	401,125

My Company Limited
INVENTORY AND WORK-IN-PROGRESS
Year ended 31 December 2012

	Draft TB €/£	Adjustments DR €/£	Adjustments (CR) €/£	31 December 2012 €/£	31 December 2011 €/£
Raw materials	44,500	10,895		55,395	40,200
Work-in-progress	19,000		(1,890)	17,110	18,100
Finished goods	21,500		(2,750)	18,750	19,500
	85,000			91,255	77,800

My Company Limited
RECEIVABLES
Year ended 31 December 2012

	Draft TB €/£	Adjustments DR €/£	Adjustments (CR) €/£	31 December 2012 €/£	31 December 2011 €/£
Trade receivables	115,400		(10,200)	105,200	101,000
Allowance for irrecoverable debts	(5,050)		(210)	(5,260)	(5,050)
	110,350			99,940	95,950
Other receivables – VAT	3,400			3,400	2,700
Prepayments – leases	1,400	100		1,500	1,400
	115,150			104,840	100,050

My Company Limited
BANK AND CASH
Year ended 31 December 2012

	Draft TB €/£	Adjustments DR €/£	Adjustments (CR) €/£	31 December 2012 €/£	31 December 2011 €/£
Bank – no. 1 account	10,323	10,200	(10,300)	10,223	10,154
Cash-in-hand	100	–	–	100	100
	10,423			10,323	10,254

My Company Limited
Payables and Accruals
Year ended 31 December 2012

	Draft TB €/£	Adjustments DR €/£	(CR) €/£	31 December 2012 €/£	31 December 2011 €/£
Trade payables	15,033		(5,500)	20,533	19,473
Other payables (Income tax)	4,700		(50,000)	54,700	103,417
Accruals	1,900		(100)	2,000	1,900
	21,633			77,233	124,790

My Company Limited
Provision for Liabilities and Charges
Year ended 31 December 2012

	Early retirement and pension costs €/£
Balance at 1 January 2012	35,000
Provision during year	15,000
Balance at 31 December 2012	50,000

My Company Limited
Revaluation Reserve
Year ended 31 December 2012

	€/£
Freehold Properties	
Balance at 1 January 2012	24,525
Arising during the year	21,000
Balance at 31 December 2012	45,525

My Company Limited
Retained Earnings
Year ended 31 December 2012

	€/£
Balance at 1 January 2012	364,914
Profit/(loss) for year	199,371
Balance at 31 December 2012	564,285

SECTION H: STATEMENT OF CASH FLOWS

My Company Limited
STATEMENT OF CASH FLOWS
Year ended 31 December 2012

Workings:

	2012 €/£
Net cash flow from operating activities	
Profit before tax	249,371
Depreciation	56,500
Amortisation	10,000
Interest charge	36,829
Loss on disposal of equipment	2,000
Increase in inventory	(13,455)
Increase in trade receivables	(3,990)
Increase in other receivables	(700)
Increase in prepayments	(100)
Increase in trade payables	1,060
Increase in accruals	100
Increase in provisions	15,000
Interest paid	(36,829)
Tax paid*	(98,717)
	217,069
Cash flows from investing activities	
Purchase of non-current assets	(219,000)
Proceeds from disposal of equipment	2,000
	(217,000)
* Tax paid	
Opening balance	103,417
Statement of comprehensive income	50,000
Closing balance	(54,700)
	98,717

Suggested Solutions to Section Four

GROUP:
POT LIMITED GROUP (POT LTD)

Solution Task 20

First Meeting with Partner and Team – Response

1. When a group is formed, there are both IFRS and legal requirements for that group to present consolidated financial statements.

IFRS Requirements IFRS 10 *Consolidated Financial Statements* states that a parent shall present consolidated financial statements in which it consolidates its investment in subsidiaries and that consolidated financial statements must include all subsidiaries of the parent.

There are certain exemptions from this requirement, the principal ones being:

(a) when the parent itself is a wholly-owned subsidiary; and/or
(b) when the parent's debt or equity instruments are not traded in a public market.

The Legal Framework In addition to preparing their own accounts, parent undertakings are required to prepare consolidated group accounts and to lay them before the annual general meeting at the same time as their own annual accounts.

In Ireland, the requirement to prepare group accounts is contained at Regulation 5 of the European Communities (Group Accounts) Regulations (S.I. 201 No. of 1992) (the GAR), and states that:

> "[A] the end of its financial year a parent undertaking shall prepare group accounts in accordance with these Regulations and such accounts shall be laid before the annual general meeting at the same time as the undertaking's annual accounts are so laid."

There are also some exemptions to the legal requirements to prepare consolidated financial statements when a parent is a private company and does not exceed certain size criteria.

In the UK, the Companies Act 2006 (section 399) states: "If at the end of a financial year the company is a parent company, the directors, as well as preparing individual accounts for the year, must prepare group accounts for the year unless the company is exempt from that requirement." **This section applies to companies that are not subject to the small companies regime.**

Under section 400, a company is exempt from the requirement to prepare group accounts if it is itself a subsidiary undertaking and its immediate parent undertaking is established under the law of a European Economic Area (EEA) state.

Under section 401, a company is exempt from the requirement to prepare group accounts if it is itself a subsidiary undertaking and its immediate parent undertaking is not established under the law of an EEA state provided certain conditions apply.

Under Section 402, a parent is exempt from the requirement to prepare group accounts if, under section 405, all of its subsidiary undertakings could be excluded from consolidation in Companies Act group accounts.

2. The criterion that determines whether a parent has acquired a subsidiary is whether the parent can *control* the other entity. IFRS 10 defines a *subsidiary* as an entity, including an unincorporated entity such as a partnership, that is **controlled** by another entity (known as the 'parent'). **Control** means having the power to govern the financial and operating policies of an entity (the subsidiary) in order to gain benefits from its activities. Control is presumed to exist when a parent owns more than 50% of the voting power of another entity. However, it can also exist when a parent does not own more than 50% of the voting power but can exercise control by, for example, an agreement with other shareholders.

3. The provisions of IAS 1 *Presentation of Financial Statements* regarding the presentation of financial statements refer both to individual financial statements and to consolidated financial statements. Indeed, the accompanying documents to IAS 1 give examples of:

   (a) a group statement of financial position;
   (b) a group statement of profit or loss and other comprehensive income; and
   (c) a group statement of changes in equity.

Items Unique to Consolidated Financial Statements

Certain items can only arise in the presentation of a consolidated statement of financial position, e.g.

- goodwill arising on consolidation is disclosed as an intangible asset;
- non-controlling interests in the subsidiary are disclosed as a separate component of equity but after owners' equity as follows:

Equity	**€/£000**
Ordinary share capital	X
Revaluation reserve	X
Retained earnings	X
Total shareholders' equity	X
Non-controlling interests	X
Total equity	X

Second Meeting with Partner and Team – Response

1. The goodwill that arose in the financial statements of the Poulenc Partnership is known as inherent goodwill, which reflects the reputation and other positive characteristics of a business, all of which are difficult to value. Inherent goodwill cannot appear in the statement of financial position which is presented under international accounting standards.

   Purchased goodwill, on the other hand, is the excess of the purchase price over the fair value of the net assets of an acquired business. Purchased goodwill can arise on consolidation and is treated as a non-current asset in the consolidated statement of financial position in accordance with IFRS 3 *Business Combinations*. Previously purchased goodwill was amortised over its economic useful life as in the case of other intangibles. In accordance with IFRS 3, it is only written down if its carrying value is impaired.

2. When a company buys the net assets of another, the acquired company is effectively liquidated and all its assets and liabilities are combined with those of the acquirer on its statement of financial position. A group is not formed. The accounting treatment is very similar to that experienced in the takeover of the Poulenc Partnership by the Poulenc Company Limited.

   When a company buys the shares of another, a different situation arises. Both companies remain in existence and continue to prepare their separate financial statements. A group is formed, which consequently requires the presentation of consolidated financial statements.

3. IFRS 10 defines non-controlling interests as the equity in a subsidiary not attributable to a parent. In more simple terms non-controlling interests is the proportion of the equity of a subsidiary owned by shareholders outside the group.

   Non-controlling interests in the net assets (capital and reserves) of consolidated subsidiaries are shown separately on the consolidated statement of financial position. The amount is shown within equity, separately from the equity of the owners of the parent as follows:

   EXTRACT FROM CONSOLIDATED STATEMENT OF FINANCIAL POSITION
   as at 31 December 2012

	€/£000
Equity	X
Ordinary share capital	X
Retained earnings	X
Total shareholders' equity	X
Non-controlling interests	X
Total equity	X

Ethical Dilemma – Response

A signed statement from the chairman is not adequate either from a company law or audit evidence perspective. Only a properly constituted board meeting of the parent could give such an undertaking.

No one individual, no matter how senior, can bind the board of directors in the manner described. After recent well-publicised cases in Ireland, e.g. regarding financial institutions, it is incumbent on audit firms to be aware of dominant personalities and their impact and influence on the audit process.

POT LTD GROUP
FINANCIAL STATEMENTS
For the year ended 30 September 2013

FILE INDEX

Section

A. Individual Statements of Financial Position of a parent (Pot Ltd) and a subsidiary (Stew Ltd)

B. Journal Entry

C. Workings for Statement of Financial Position using the T Account Method

D. Workings for Statement of Financial Position using the Columnar Method

E. Consolidated Statement of Financial Position

SECTION A: INDIVIDUAL STATEMENTS OF FINANCIAL POSITION

Statements of Financial Position of a Parent (Pot Ltd) and its Subsidiary Stew Ltd
as at 30 September 2013

	Pot €/£000	Stew €/£000
Assets		
Non-current assets		
Property, plant and equipment	5,600	2,160
Investment in Stew	1,260	0
Non-current assets		
Inventory	290	220
Trade receivables	330	250
Bank and cash	100	60
Total Assets	**7,580**	**2,690**
Equity and Liabilities		
Equity		
Ordinary share capital	4,000	1,000
Revaluation reserve	0	200
Retained earnings	3,010	1,050
Total equity	7,010	2,250
Non-current liabilities		
Trade payables	570	440
Total Equity and Liabilities	**7,580**	**2,690**

Relevant information:

1. Pot acquired 800,000 ordinary shares in Stew on 1 December 2010 when the retained earnings of Stew amounted to €/£550,000.
2. During September 2013 Stew sold goods to Pot at invoice value €/£150,000 on which the selling company earned a margin of 20%. One half of these goods was in the inventory of Pot at the reporting date.
3. The revaluation reserve arose in the year under review following a professional valuation of the property plant and equipment of Stew Ltd.

Guidance Note

The workings involved in the preparation of consolidated financial statements occupy approximately 95% of the total time allotted to answering an examination question on this topic. However, if a question requires, for example, the presentation of a consolidated statement of financial position, you must enter the figures derived from your workings. Failure to achieve this would result in a significant loss of marks even if your workings are 100% accurate.

> *Key Point* When preparing a consolidated statement of financial position, the investment in a subsidiary (in the individual statement of financial position of the parent) is replaced by the net assets of that subsidiary.

Consolidated Statement of Financial Position Workings

Many lecturers and students prefer the T account method for workings, while others are in favour of the columnar method. This section will show the workings under both methods which will result in an identical consolidated statement of financial position. Choose your preferred method and stick with it.

Solution Notes

1. The group structure must be calculated and should always be shown. The structure is based on the number of shares in the subsidiary owned by the parent (the group) and the non-controlling interests. Thus, Pot owns 800,000 of the 1 million shares in issue by Stew, or 80%. The non-controlling interests therefore own 20%.
2. In accordance with IFRS 10, all the assets and liabilities of a subsidiary are consolidated with those of the parent. This principle is known as 'full consolidation' and applies whether the subsidiary is wholly owned by the parent or less than wholly owned, e.g. 75%.
3. Goodwill is calculated by comparing:

    (a) what the parent paid for its investment in the subsidiary, i.e. the cost of the investment in the statement of financial position of the parent; and
    (b) what the parent got for its investment, i.e. its share of the share capital and reserves (or net assets) of the subsidiary at the date of acquisition.

4. Non-controlling interests are credited with their share of the share capital and reserves (net assets) of the subsidiary at the reporting date.

SECTION B: JOURNAL ENTRY

		€/£000	€/£000

Journal 1   Debit   Retained earnings (selling company) Stew   15
             Credit Inventory   15
             With the unrealised inventory profit
             €/£150,000 × 20% × ½

SECTION C: WORKINGS – T ACCOUNT METHOD

WORKINGS

Property, Plant and Equipment

	€/£000		€/£000
Pot	5,600		
Stew	2,160	Consol. SoFP	7,760
	7,760		7,760

Investment in Stew

	€/£000		€/£000
Pot	1,260	Cost of control	1,260

Inventory

	€/£000		€/£000
Pot	290	Journal 1	15
Stew	220	Consol. SoFP	495
	510		510

Trade Receivables

	€/£000		€/£000
Pot	330		
Stew	250	Consol. SoFP	580
	580		580

Bank and Cash

	€/£000		€/£000
Pot	100		
Stew	60	Consol. SoFP	160
	160		160

Trade Payables

	€/£000		€/£000
		Pot	570
Consol. SoFP	1,010	Stew	440
	1,010		1,010

Note: The ordinary shares of Stew must be apportioned according to the group structure and transferred to cost of control and non-controlling interests accordingly. The share capital of Pot is also the share capital of the group.

Ordinary Shares

	€/£000		€/£000
Cost of control (80%)	800	Pot	4,000
NCI (20%)	200	Stew	1,000
Consol. SoFP	4,000		
	5,000		5,000

Each reserve of Stew must be apportioned as follows:

- Cost of control is credited with the group's share of the balance at **acquisition date**.
- NCI is credited with their share at the **reporting date**.
- The revaluation reserve of Stew arose during the year under review. Therefore, there was no balance at the date of acquisition.

Revaluation Reserve

	€/£000		€/£000
Cost of control	0	Stew	200
NCI (20% x 200)	40		
Consol. SoFP	160		
	200		200

Retained Earnings

	€/£000		€/£000
Journal 1 (Stew)	15	Pot	3,010
Cost of control	440	Stew	1,050
(80% x 550)			
NCI	207		
20% (1,050 – 15)*			
Consol. SoFP	3,398		
	4,060		4,060

* The retained earnings of Stew at the reporting date (1,050) are reduced by the adjustment for the unrealised inventory profit (15) as Stew was the selling company.

Cost of Control

	€/£000		€/£000
Investment in Stew	1,260	Ord. shares Stew	800
		Ret. earnings Stew	440
		Goodwill	20
	1,260		1260

Non-controlling Interests (NCI)

	€/£000		€/£000
		Ord. shares Stew	200
Consol. SoFP	447	Reval. reserve Stew	40
		Ret. earnings Stew	207
	447		447

SECTION D: WORKINGS – COLUMNAR METHOD

WORKINGS

	Pot €/£000	Stew €/£000	Adjustments €/£000	Consol. SoFP €/£000
Property, plant and equipment	5,600	2,160		7,760
Investment in Stew	1,260		(1,260)	0
Goodwill (W1)			20	20
Inventory	290	220	(15)	495
Trade receivables	330	250		580
Bank and cash	100	60		160
Total Assets	**7,580**	**2,690**	**(1,255)**	**9,015**
Ordinary shares	4,000	1,000	(1000)	4,000
Revaluation reserve (W2)	200		(40)	160
Retained earnings (W3)	3,010	1,050	(662)	3,398
Non-controlling interests (W4)			447	447
Trade payables	570	440		1,010
Total Equity and Liabilities	**7,580**	**2,690**	**(1,255)**	**9,015**

(W1) Goodwill	€/£000	€/£000
Cost of investment		1,260
Stew at acquisition date		
Ordinary shares	1,000	
Retained earnings	550	
	1,550 × 80%	1,240
Goodwill		20

(W2) Revaluation reserve
Stew   200
Less non-controlling interests 20%   (40)
Consol. SoFP   160

(W3) Retained earnings
Pot at reporting date   3,010
Stew
At reporting date   1,050
Unrealised inventory profit   (15)
     1,035
At acquisition date   550
Post-acquisition   485 × 80%   388
Consol. SoFP   3,398

(W4) Non-controlling interests

	€/£000	€/£000
Stew at reporting date		
Ordinary shares	1,000	
Revaluation reserve	200	
Retained earnings	1,050	
Unrealised inventory profit	(15)	
	2,235 × 20%	447